MATT ANDERSEN

COMPLETING

THE

DEAL

AN INSIDE LOOK AT MERGERS,

ACQUISITIONS, AND RAISING CAPITAL

RIVER GROVE
BOOKS

Published by River Grove Books
Austin, TX
www.rivergrovebooks.com

Distributed by River Grove Books

Design and composition by Greenleaf Book Group and Teresa Muñiz
Cover design by Greenleaf Book Group and Teresa Muñiz
Cover images used under license from ©Shutterstock/Miloje

Publisher's Cataloging-in-Publication data is available.

Print ISBN: 978-1-63299-691-6

eBook ISBN: 978-1-63299-692-3

First Edition

This book is dedicated to all the founders and company owners we have worked with over the years. Though we may have taught them something about business transactions, they have taught us about the dedication, passion, and drive for success that can turn a raw idea into an exciting journey of growth and ultimately a legacy.

CONTENTS

Contents

PREFACE

During my years as an investment banker and advisor, I have spent a lot of time working for companies that utilized capital to grow organically, acquire other businesses, and sometimes both. Capital raising, growth, acquisitions, and liquidity are some of the most challenging yet rewarding projects an entrepreneur can experience, and I have been fortunate to accompany many business leaders on these journeys.

After 24 years in the business, closing over $5 billion in securities, debt, and mergers and acquisitions (M&A), there have been many lessons. Some were learned the easy way; some not so much. I've been a part of more than 150 securities, debt, restructuring, and M&A transactions and observed more than twice that. Having witnessed so many of these transactions, it seems like one should be able to point to an exact process to follow—a formula that would always result in a "successful" result, whatever the desired outcome. If only.

In all of the mergers and acquisitions my firm and I have participated in, and as I've advised countless CEOs and boards, there are no guarantees of a successful outcome. There are no completely predictable outcomes, and there are complexities in every situation, with every scenario different and every outcome unique. There are also valuable variables with valued opinions—the people involved in growing, shaping, and evolving the company each with individual needs, interests, and goals.

At the beginning of many new client relationships, when the ink is still drying on our engagement terms and intros are still being made, we have a "kickoff" meeting to start our new client-advisor relationship. It's then that I hear, "What is the likelihood of success for this deal?" In nine out of every ten meetings with new clients, we hear this question, in so many words. And I'll tell you what we tell them.

My answer is, "No deal is the same; each takes on a life of its own during the process. We can point to things we know work well, and things we know don't. However, the variables in the process far outweigh the fixed elements."

Don't get me wrong—it's not a bad question. It's one most people would probably ask as well. This book is meant to highlight options, strategies, and proven concepts that we've seen work to improve your odds of completing the right transaction.

The answer is always, "No deal is the same." No business is exactly like another, no matter how many similarities. You'll see this with even some of the most well-known coffee chains in the world. What might work 100 percent of the time on one side of the street may only work 50 percent of the time on the other, or even less—even with the same products, service, and process. You get the picture.

While there is no silver bullet or easy button for success, there are approaches and steps to get you 90 percent of the way there. After years of transactions, I started to see patterns and repetition and began to take note of what works and what does not work. At Westlake Securities, our Investment Banking firm in Texas, we utilize these experiences to formulate strategies to help clients think through some of the issues that come with growing, exiting, or buying a company—strategies that will be shared with you in these pages.

This book was written so readers like you can benefit from my experience and hopefully not have to learn the hard way. You'll have to tailor my advice to your own circumstances, but what you'll read in this book may save you many needless headaches and give you an advantage in the face of new opportunities and challenging situations.

This book is meant to be a practical companion to CEOs, entrepreneurs, and board members who want to see their companies through these various scenarios to prosper and achieve greater success. However, it is not meant to be a DIY book, but rather a helpful guide along the way of a professional transactional process. The real-life stories and day-to-day occurrences included in this book offer practical "Main Street" advice—advice for navigating various situations, for attracting Wall Street-caliber capital, and most importantly, making advantageous deals.

The goal of this book is to help better prepare you for big strategic questions, discussions, and decisions. Does your company stay the same? Does it grow exponentially? Should it bring on capital? Should you sell? Once you decide what to do, how do you effectively begin that process?

INTRODUCTION

L et's start from the beginning and take a foundational look at business operations that succeed. To operate any company you need four things.

First, you need customers. Who is buying your product or service? In consumer markets, people will buy your product either because they *need* to, such as food and clothing, or because they *want* to, such as a wide-screen TV or a powerboat. If your customers are other businesses, they aren't buying something because they want to, but because they have a problem for which you have the solution—new software, a piece of equipment, or an innovative strategy.

Second, you need a product or service to sell. Customers will buy it from you because it solves a problem. Your product must be of high quality and sold at a fair price.

Third, you need mechanisms with which to make your products and sell them. This is your business. It includes yourself, your employees, and your board members, as well as physical tools, such as your software, consumable product, factory, retail store, website, and supply chain.

Finally, after you've got customers, products or services to sell, and mechanisms with which to make your products and sell them, you need a platform for the exchange/transaction. As the purpose of every company is to be engaged in commerce (which in our modern era means the exchange of money), the ultimate goal is to earn, through sales of your product or service to your customers, more money than it costs to create and operate the company. If you keep earning more than you spend, your business is growing. Sounds simple and straightforward enough. Dream. Plan. Execute. Sell. Grow.

Now what?

This is where we typically enter the picture. Let's say Company X has been developed by its founder and leader, "Clyde," who's done an incredible job of tripling the business in ten years. He's organically grown the business tenfold, with little outside help, and is thinking, *What now? What's that next level of growth and how do we get there?*

Clyde considers his options. Should he raise capital—acquire an infusion of capital from some external source? Should he merge with, acquire, or sell to another firm to create a bigger company? Having successfully grown the business for many years, and since it's privately owned, Clyde will eventually need to start thinking about an exit plan. At what point or level of success might he want to sell the company? Clyde could sell, take the capital, retire to a desirable location, and focus on hobbies. Or he could reinvest capital into a new company and take it to the next level of growth before selling.

In 2002, when Elon Musk sold PayPal to eBay for $1.5 billion, he took the $180 million he received from the sale and invested it into SpaceX ($100 million), Tesla ($70 million), and SolarCity ($10 million). In early 2021, Tesla was worth $830 billion, and Elon Musk ranked number seven on the Forbes 400 list of the wealthiest people in the world. Not too bad—even if later events saw part of his fortune melt away.

Some exit strategies aren't exits at all. In Japan, there's been a strong tradition of family ownership for generations. The oldest family business in the world is a Japanese hot springs resort hotel, Nishiyama Onsen Keiunkan, in Hayakawa, Yamanashi Prefecture, Japan. Founded in 705 CE by Fujiwara Mahito, for over 1,300 years it has been continuously operated by 52 generations of the same family, including adopted heirs.

You probably don't foresee your company staying in your family for 13 centuries—but it's nice to know it's possible.

Back to Clyde. He's successfully grown the business and kept enough cash flow to cover the essentials—equipment, transportation, employees, etc. But as he looks to further grow, what if he wants to expand his product portfolio? Where is that capital coming from? What does the cash flow cycle look like? Given that the cash flow cycle often takes months—or years, in some cases—to get the targeted return on investment, there could be times when no cash flow is being generated from the company; instead, cash flow is being reinvested to produce services or products at higher levels. If the growth is significant and the cash flow cycle is too long or the growth plan hits a hiccup, the company can die of capital starvation.

Many founders want to exponentially expand their business to meet a significant projected increase in demand. Then it's like starting all over again—they need to find capital, invest it, and then collect the return of their investment over a multiyear period.

Like everything else your company needs, if you need to get capital from the outside, it will come at a price. If you borrow money, you'll need to pay it back with interest. If you accept an equity investment in your company, then the investor becomes a part owner and is entitled to a share of a portion of the company if, for example, it is sold or later recapitalized.

This book is about business financing—the types of capital, the cost and complexity of it, and how to prepare and manage an exit. It's written for company owners and other stakeholders who aren't experts in finance. You can hire experts to assist you, but you must be conversant in the language and business of finance. It's part of the CEO job description to understand your company's options, the benefits and drawbacks, and be able to recognize when the advice you're getting is sound. After all, it's your money, your company, and no one will care about it as much as you do.

HOW THIS BOOK IS ORGANIZED

We start with the basics and work our way through, step by step. The first chapter delves into the concept of capital and where you can find it, from banks to crowdsourcing services. We then discuss in chapter 2 how you can apply the cash you've sourced—the various types and uses of capital, such as senior debt, junior debt, and equity. Each strategy has its advantages and disadvantages, and when you consult with your financial advisors, you need to be up to speed on what they might recommend to you.

In chapter 3, we cover mergers and acquisitions and, not surprisingly, how to arrive at an accurate valuation. To give you a solid understanding of the potential benefits and pitfalls, we'll unravel knotty subjects, including timing, terms and conditions, auctions, and how to select an investment bank. We'll also discuss roll-up mergers and acquisition strategies.

In chapter 4, we talk about the deal—which leads up to the moment you sign on the dotted line. Here's where the rubber meets the road, and where many founders transacting for the first time get hung up. The book will guide you through the various stages, including why you'd want to make an acquisition (or be acquired), intellectual property, market share issues, the regulatory environment, and much more.

Why would a target company want to sell? There could be any one of many reasons—high market activity driving up prices, the retirement of the owner, competitive business headwinds, or for financial conditions. It's important for you to see clearly because the key drivers affecting the sale will be known by most buyers.

When it's time for a sale, you need to know how to prepare for it, and chapter 5 lays out the details so you'll be ready when the time comes. This includes creating defensibility, readying your management team, organizing your diligence materials, and other steps that will help to make the process as smooth as possible. The goal is to get the very best execution in your sales process that you can for your company—and this book will help you do that.

Among other insights, you'll learn how to avoid deal-killing statements, such as bringing up unknown risk that has not been discussed, macro trends moving against the industry, or an unclear growth path. Instead, you'll want to focus on deal-selling statements, such as showing that the projected growth of the business is clear, realistic, and concise, with stats and figures to back up statements. Effective communication is key.

Know that making a deal happen can and typically will take time, and in the journey to the all-important closing, mistakes can be made. Chapter 6 shows you how to stay on track, avoid "deal fatigue," and develop the mentality that it takes to get a transaction across the finish line. Then, in chapter 7, you'll learn what happens after the close, including how to follow your operating plan and, perhaps most importantly, how to adjust to change. Your company has been your life's work, and it can be hard to accept that it will change. You should set an example for management to handle this change with grace and flexibility.

To make these complex issues as simple as possible, at the end of the book there are convenient Appendices that include a wealth of checklists. You'll find Key Ratios and Terms, a Growth Capital Guidelines Checklist, and a detailed Due Diligence Checklist that you can use as a road map to a successful deal.

Ready? Let's get started.

Chapter 1

MODERN HISTORY OF CAPITAL

E very company begins with three things: an idea, work, and capital. Most entrepreneurs, from Henry Ford to Oprah Winfrey, have no shortage of ideas, nor are they hesitant to put in the work necessary to succeed.

Starting out, every entrepreneur needs *capital* to cover initial expenses to get the company started—to pay for equipment, raw materials, employees, office space, and so on. They also need cash to cover revenue shortfalls. The amount of capital depends on the industry.

Regardless of the amount of capital needed and regardless of timing, the important questions become: "How many dollars?" and "On what terms?"—or in other words, "At what price?"

Today, business owners have access to many sources of capital. Like many aspects of modern-day life, the past several decades have been hallmarked by innovations, efficiency, ease of business and daily life, and ever-expanding opportunities to connect, learn, and grow. The private financial markets have shared this fascinating path as well. Access to capital (and capital providers) has never been more efficient than it is right now with thousands of banks, private credit, equity, and family office investors and buyers.

That being said, it is still not easy and is not without its quirks. Let's look at some of the sources of capital for a company.

BANKS

Modern banking has progressed from offering only a narrow window of commercial loans to the largest companies to now include specialty programs, financing alternatives, and other creative programs that are essential to modern-day, middle-market company growth and mergers and acquisitions. Programs like the Small Business Administration (SBA), U.S. Department of Agriculture (USDA) opportunity zones, employee stock ownership plans (ESOP), and institutional lending groups that didn't exist 40 years ago are now common components of the modern landscape of business financing. Additionally, the types of loans that the "right" middle-market lenders provide reach far beyond traditional commercial real estate mortgages and sleepy revolving lines of credit. Term loans, cash flow loans, and other finance structures have given senior debt an ever-expanding importance in growth and M&A considerations.

With $23.6 trillion of assets, commercial banks in the United States comprise the largest segment of available capital.[1]

Many of our clients ask if this is a preferred path. The answer is simple: There is no one path that is going to work for every situation. Companies should view a capital raise strategically and determine which route is best. Bank financing is ideal for middle market companies that are fairly established and have a strong base of assets. Banks can typically offer the least expensive forms of capital, but there are limitations that come with that. Banks predominately want to do two things: provide liquidity for illiquidity and/or lend on a multiple of cash flow.

A few years ago, a family office in the Midwest that specializes in iconic food brands was looking to expand and complement its portfolio of offerings—to grow its revenue footprint through customer synergies and manage all financing needs and operational expenses through holding company synergies. We will call our Midwest Family Office "FamilyFoods."

We were able to recommend and get a senior credit facility with a prominent bank for FamilyFoods to acquire an iconic company that was in its seventh decade of business, had a solid reputation for quality, a strong leadership team, highly trained employees, and excellent logistics and shipping systems in place. Not to mention, it was (and still is) one of the most well-known brands in its industry. The transaction made sense for the bank lender, given the rich and established history of the iconic confection/snack company. The products,

....

1 United States—Total Assets, All Commercial Banks," Trading Economics, https://tradingeconomics.com/united-states/total-assets-all-commercial-banks-fed-data.html.

business practices, loyal and ongoing customers, supply chain, and incredibly strong market position were all well beyond proven after 70 years.

This transaction was financed by a majority of the capital coming from a bank lender in the form of leveraged buyout ("LBO") financing, and it allowed the buyer maximum capital efficiency and minimal capital outlay. This type of transaction is very common in the private equity world, and many founders are surprised when they learn what is possible when working with the "right" parts of a bank today.

PRIVATE EQUITY AND VENTURE CAPITAL

Far and away, this group has seen the most change in recent years. The Private Equity and Venture Capital markets were created to provide increased returns over publicly traded securities by investing in private companies. They help to create liquidity for business interests that would otherwise be illiquid and provide capital for organic and inorganic growth. The reason why private equity, in particular, has had such a surge in activity over the last few years is due to the realization that 80 percent of all privately held businesses are family or founder owned. But of these, only 30 percent will attempt to transition to the second generation and 12 percent to the third generation.

Along the way, there becomes a need for both liquidity and leadership change. There are also life-cycle considerations, where it may make sense for a family or founder to no longer own and control a company and instead transfer it to the hands of others, and seek liquidity in exchange for that transaction. That's where private equity plays a role in terms of offering liquidity and succession management.

The formalization of this group's existence has been nothing short of prolific. Groups like Apollo, KKR, Blackstone, Sequoia and Carlyle have paved the way for all sorts of early-stage venture capital through Large Cap Buyout funds and funds that exist on the spectrum in between. Recent figures show that private equity has over $1.96 trillion to invest in the United States, and venture capital groups have an additional $298.5 billion.[2] Just a few decades ago, these options were much more thinly available or were nonexistent to founders when compared to today. Today's founders or company owners have access to capital tools that never existed before.

PRIVATE CREDIT FUNDS

Also referred to as *direct lending* or *private lending*, private credit is an asset defined by non-bank lending in which the debt is not issued or traded on the public markets.

Business development companies (BDCs) are a form of closed-end investment companies in the United States that invest in medium- to large-sized businesses.

Similar to venture capital (VC) or private equity (PE) funds, BDCs provide investors with a way to invest in private companies and benefit from the sale of those investments. But while VC and PE funds are

....

2   Kia Kokalitcheva, "Venture Capital Has Lots of Dry Powder in 2023," Axios, January 14,
      2023, https://www.axios.com/2023/01/14/venture-capital-dry-powder-2023; Dylan
      Thomas, "Global Private Equity Dry Powder Approaches $2 Trillion," S&P Global,
      December 21, 2022, https://www.spglobal.com/marketintelligence/en/news-insights/
      latest-news-headlines/global-private-equity-dry-powder-approaches-2-trillion-73570292.

often closed to all but very wealthy investors, BDCs typically allow anyone to purchase shares through their publicly traded equity.

After the Great Recession, private credit and debt funds saw an upswing, going from $311.7 billion of assets in December of 2010 to an estimated $1.25 trillion as of mid-2022.[3] These funds have a significant advantage over banks in their ability to lend creatively. While the cost of borrowing is higher than at a bank, many deals made in the last 10 years would not have happened without this group of capital providers.

FAMILY OFFICES

Family offices have a long and colorful history. In 15th-century Florence, the Medici family used its wealth to actively support young artists by investing in their works, a form of patronage that underwrote the works of some of the greatest masters of all time, from Michelangelo and Leonardo Da Vinci to Galileo and Botticelli. The Medici Bank, from its creation in 1397 to its demise in 1494, was one of the most respected and prosperous institutions in Europe, and among the earliest businesses to use the double-entry bookkeeping system for tracking credits and debits.

In the United States, the Rockefeller family pioneered family offices in the late 19th century. Family offices traditionally have

....

3   Treabhor Mac Eochaidh, "Private Debt: Global Market Opportunities," *Prequin*, July 12, 2022, https://www.preqin.com/insights/research/quarterly-updates/private-debt-q2-2022#:~:text=The%20growth%20of%20private%20credit%20assets%2C%20an%20estimated,drove%20that%20growth%20are%20beginning%20to%20show%20up.

worked funds of all sorts and are currently active in the investment world. Over the past few years, they have been pursuing direct investment stakes. Between 2010 and 2015, direct investment by family offices surged over 200 percent and has continued to rise through the early 2020s.[4] A large portion of this growth can be attributed to newer family offices formed since 2015. About two-thirds of these newer family offices are investing directly, compared to about half of family offices formed between 2006 and 2010 and only 25 percent of those founded before 1985.[5] Family offices are free from many of the constraints and conflicts that the previously mentioned capital partners have, making them an attractive pool of capital to work with.

INSURANCE COMPANIES

The insurance industry entered the private capital markets at their inception. With the need for yield and return coupled with long horizon times, private equity and lending are a natural fit for insurance companies' investments. Due to this strategic match, insurance companies can finance long-term improvement projects, such as helping farmers to buy land and farming equipment or developing municipal infrastructure like commercial and multifamily properties. This large amount of investment can help to solidify the capital

....

4   Rebecca Hinds and Anne Gherini, "The Rise of Family Office Direct and Co-Investing," *affinity*, accessed February 2023, https://www.affinity.co/blog/family-offices-direct-investing.

5   Hinds and Gherini, "The Rise of Family Office."

markets. The assets of insurance companies total nearly $6 trillion and account for 21 percent of corporate bonds and 20 percent of municipal bonds.[6]

CROWDFUNDING AND INVESTMENT NETWORKS

Nowadays, there are many ways to connect with accredited investors through investment groups and crowdfunding sites. These groups allow companies that are typically early stage to connect with groups of accredited investors who help fund their visions.

It seems like an easy process: You sign up with a high-quality crowdfunding platform, list your funding needs, click a few buttons, and the money comes pouring in. Of course, it's *not* that easy, and nothing's guaranteed. Like any fundraising or marketing campaign, you need a smart strategy and solid execution.

The most successful categories of crowdfunding campaigns are video games, films, and computer software or hardware projects. But you never know—fundraising for an old-fashioned card game called "Exploding Kittens" hit $1 million in just eight hours on Kickstarter—and eventually reached over $8.7 million.

Investment networks are pretty much exactly what they sound like: loosely associated groups of people who invest in small businesses. For example, Angel Investment Network was founded in

....

6   Center for Capital Markets Competitiveness, "The Role of Insurance Investments in the U.S. Economy," Spring 2019, 4, https://www.centerforcapitalmarkets.com/resource/the-role-of-insurance-investments-in-the-u-s-economy/.

2004 by two people in the United Kingdom who wanted to make an online platform for connecting startups with a global network of angel investors. By 2021, it had 30 branches extending to 80 different countries, with more than 1.9 million registered members, 318,000 investors, and over 1.6 million entrepreneurs.[7]

PRIVATE EQUITY VERSUS INDEPENDENT SPONSOR VERSUS CREDIT FUNDS

So what are the subtleties in private equity, independent sponsors, and private credit? It's important to understand the differences between them and what might ultimately be the right fit in your capital or liquidity search.

Private equity typically raises what is called a *committed capital fund*, meaning they have established certain parameters for the size of the fund, the investment verticals, check-size structure, and return profile. It also means they have already started a conversation with a desirable pool of institutional investors, such as pension funds, investment managers, endowments, and insurance companies, and have raised the capital to be invested in their strategy. The strategy is typically designed to play to the strengths of the managers and the team behind them. The fund will typically have anywhere from $50 million to well over $1 billion and will typically run a life cycle of gathering and investing in the fund assets over a period of three years. The focus

....

7 "About Us," The USA Angel Investment Network, https://www.angelinvestmentnetwork.us/about-us#:~:text=We%20have%201%2C914%2C587%20registered%20members,USA%20and%20across%20the%20world.

then shifts to realizing the value of those investments by selling the businesses or liquidating their positions by the end of 10 years and returning capital to their investors. Now the dedicated funds have new capital to invest.

Independent sponsors are people who likely have a loose network of investors and will do transactions on a case-by-case basis. Typically, when a company agrees to a transaction with them, the independent sponsor then turns to their investor base to raise the capital in order to get the transaction closed. They typically do not have dedicated funds, nor do they typically have dedicated capital to get a deal done on their own. They are usually using other people's money.

Both approaches work in a fairly similar way and typically get paid in a combination of three ways:

One way is a *cash administrative fee*. This fee may be a monthly or quarterly fee that gets paid to the administration and supervisors of the investment, and it usually comes from the company.

The second way is through an *asset management fee*, which can range from 1 to 2 percent of the assets. So, for example, if they buy a company that is worth $30 million, they typically get paid 1.5 percent on top of that $30 million to manage those assets.

Last but not least is *carried interest*. Carried interest is similar to a stock grant that has certain performance minimums before it actually has value. Typically, a carried interest structure will say that the management group overseeing the asset, the private equity group, or the independent sponsor will get 20 percent of the return after investors have received an 8 percent minimum return. It is an interesting and attractive model for both the investor and the company.

Credit funds are composed of a series of limited partners or investors and work in a similar way to private equity in terms of raising and deploying capital over a limited period of time, but they might recycle the capital more quickly than a private equity group would. They will return capital at the end of a fund cycle, which may be somewhat shorter than an equity cycle—often seven years instead of 10, as an example. Those funds typically get paid the same way: either an administrative fee, an asset management fee from investors, or carried interest from investors.

In summary, there are several groups that provide capital to meet the needs of companies based on various stages and maturity levels. These groups will become important to understand as we work through the upcoming chapters on capital planning, structure, and desired outcomes.

Chapter 2

TYPES AND USES OF CAPITAL

Capital is one of the greatest votes of confidence a company can get from a third party. It demonstrates that a third party is willing to lend its funds, invest equity, and perhaps even ultimately own the entirety of the business.

SENIOR DEBT

When we look at capital, we will refer to *senior debt* as being number one, as it is the most widely used form of debt in the United States. Senior debt means debt and obligations that, in the case of borrower bankruptcy, are prioritized for repayment. If the borrower is forced to liquidate, senior debt has the highest priority and therefore is often considered the lowest risk to the lender/investor.

This capital typically comes from a commercial bank. There are various forms of debt that exist in this range, from small, guaranteed lines of credit to SBA loans and all the way to USDA loans as the deal size increases. Cash flow loans and other sophisticated forms of financing also use senior debt. Senior debt also can come in the form of non-bank debt, which typically lends itself more to credit funds and factoring, which we will discuss as well.

JUNIOR AND MEZZANINE DEBT

Junior debt is a second lien form of capital that lives between senior debt and equity. It refers to bonds or other forms of debt issued that, in the case of default, have a lower priority for repayment than other, more senior debt claims. Because of this, junior debt tends to be riskier for investors and thus carries higher interest rates than more senior debt from the same issuer. It is usually provided by credit funds for businesses that are doing $2 million or more of EBITDA (Earnings Before Interest, Taxes, Depreciation, and Amortization) and is typically utilized for growth purposes or leveraged buyout opportunities.

Junior debt is closely related to mezzanine debt. While there are differences, the terms are increasingly being used interchangeably. Mezzanine debt generally seeks to get both a cash payment in the form of interest and an equity upside participation via warrants. Warrants are a form of equity, and for the most part, those warrants will have a strike price of $.01, and when exercised, they typically convert into common equity.

As a simple example, let's say that ABC Company owes Bank X $50 million in the senior position and Credit Fund Y $20 million in the junior position. To compensate for the differences in risk, ABC Company pays a higher interest rate to Credit Fund Y (the junior) than to Bank X (the senior). Unfortunately, ABC Company goes bankrupt and must be liquidated. The sale nets $60 million. The senior lender, Bank X, will be paid first and in full—$50 million. The junior lender, Credit Fund Y, will receive only $10 million. The difference in security interest creates a difference in cost profile.

UNITRANCHE DEBT

Before we move on to equity, let's look at a hybrid form of debt that combines both junior and senior debt into a single tranche of capital called a *unitranche*. This debt essentially combines the forces, opportunities, and amounts of the senior debt and junior debt into a single tranche with a single, stated interest rate. There are several other facets to both senior and junior debt that we will cover in depth in later chapters. A few of these facets include terms of interest rates and both current pay and cash pay. Additionally, a unitranche debt structure may have a dilutive security called warrants that are attached to junior debt or mezzanine debt and enhance the return to the investor but dilute the shareholders.

EQUITY

There are typically two major categories of equity: *preferred stock* and *common equity*.

Preferred stock usually sits as the most senior form of equity. Preferred stockholders have a higher claim to dividends or asset distribution than common stockholders, and in the event of a liquidation, a preferred stockholder's claim on assets is greater than that of common stockholders but less than that of bondholders.

Preferred stock is used in many different types of deals, such as venture capital or private equity. It is generally favored over common stock because of the unique features that can be attached to it. Some of those features include preferences, liquidation preferences, investor rights, and dividends. It is for these reasons that preferred stock is one of the major forms of capital from outside parties such as venture capitalists, private equity, and others.

Common stock is the most common form of equity among founder-owned businesses that have not received outside capital or outside investment, or family-owned businesses that may be internally owned by family members. It is one of the least common forms when it comes to bringing in outside, third-party capital. In those instances, common stock is usually the last form of capital to get paid. It is typically left as incentive compensation or rollover equity.

To understand the preferences, let's walk through a quick transaction. In the event of the liquidation of a company, senior debt is going to have a first lien priority and will get paid before all others. Junior debt or mezzanine debt would have the next level of priority given their second lien status, and they are typically the next to get paid out. Following that, preferred stockholders will get their payout. Lastly, the common stockholders get paid.

These are the capital forms that can be utilized in a company's capital structure. There are, of course, different subcategories, such as structured equity, for instance. Structured equity is special in that it is a form of equity that blends itself in between debt and equity. It typically has features of debt, such as repayment, but also has features of equity, allowing for flexible repayment and a defined return profile.

Types of Capital Raising and Relevant Metrics/Characteristics

	ABL	1st Lien	Unitranche	Mezzanine	Structured Equity	Preferred Equity	Common Equity
Lien/Security	1st Lien	1st Lien	1st Lien	2nd Lien	2nd Lien/ None	None	None
Characteristics	Secure by hard assets	Cash flow based with level of asset coverage	Cash flow based with levels of asset coverage	Cash flow based	Cash flow based with line of sight to liquidity event	Liquidity event based	Liquidity event based
Key Ratio	LTV	Debt: EBITDA	Debt: EBITDA	Debt: EBITDA	Debt: EV	EV	EV
Usage Ratio	65% to 120% LTV	2.5x-3.5x EBITDA	2.5x-5x EBITDA	1.0x-2.5x EBITDA	N/A	N/A	N/A
Total Leverage	65% to 120% LTV	2.5x-3.5x EBITDA	2.5x-5x EBITDA	1.0x-2.5x EBITDA	N/A	N/A	N/A
Amortization	2 to 20 years	3 to 10 years	3 to 20 years	3 to 20 years	3 to 10 years	N/A	N/A
Warrants	N/A	N/A	Likely	Highly likely	Likely	N/A	N/A
Equity Co-Invest	N/A	N/A	Likely	Highly likely	N/A	N/A	N/A
Example Pricing	5.5% to 8.5%	6.5% to 8.5%	9% to 15%	10 to 15%	20% IRR+	20% IRR+	30% IRR+

USES OF CAPITAL

As a company moves through different cycles, understanding the role that capital can play in each cycle is critical. The five major cycles on which we'll be focusing are startup, expansion, maturity, acquisition, and distress or decline. We will cover each one of these topics in great depth and will focus on businesses that have achieved a level of earnings before interest, taxes, depreciation, and amortization (EBITDA) of at least $2.0 million.

In the upcoming chapters, we cover the key highlights of getting a deal done in the capital markets and will stress, in a summarized condensed format, the things that every CEO should know in terms of how their business relates to capital. We also discuss how understanding the capital markets and being able to get a capital market deal done impacts the evolution of a company and the creation of wealth for its shareholders.

Seeking capital for growth is a unique process, and because there is rarely a "solve all" solution, it's best addressed on a company-by-company basis. However, there are commonalities in the process that need to be present in order to achieve a successful growth-capital raise. Those commonalities are best described with the analogy of building a bridge and the concept of going from point A to point B while reducing the risk along the way. The goal is that a capital raise pitch and presentation should remove the rope and wooden planks and replace them with concrete and steel. It's the only way investors or buyers ever get comfortable, and it's a healthy and helpful process for the company to go through.

The first goal of raising growth capital is to find the best partner for the company. This "best partner" scenario generally means that, beyond capital, the culture or skill set of the capital provider matches well with where the company is currently and where it is going. It is important to have a distinguished, well-constructed presentation and thought process from the start. From the type of capital needed to operational and financial plans, the capital request that results in success is the one that is best constructed.

Non-Ideal Scenario

- Light or overly aggressive financial modeling
- Lack of cash flow "gap" or "depth" understanding
- Unknown timeliness and visibility where revenue will come from
- Lack of clarity on method or payback or investor return

Capital In
"Beginning Point"

Capital Out
"Ending Point"

Abyss of Unknown Risk

Many capital raises are centered around three occurrences— three reasons for needing the funding—that pay varying amounts of attention to strategy, modeling, and information to complete a successful raise:

1. Short-term order/project finance—single or short-term occurrence that results in a large order, product push, or single project that expands revenue but is generally not viewed as recurring

2. Long-term expansion—growth that requires both capital and operational expenditures to meet an overall market demand that is expanding and predicted to continue for several years, thus recurring in nature

3. Acquisition—buyout of the assets or stock in a competitor, vendor, or "new skill" company

The following components are critical to a successful campaign to raise growth capital. They are valuable to all stakeholders, and if done correctly, position the raise for success:

- **Defining the strategy and opportunity**. What has created the capital need? What is the opportunity and what is the capital needed to execute?

- **Performance and current position**. How has the company performed in the recent past? Why or how is the company in a position to capitalize on growth opportunities?

- **Current and future capital structures**. What is the current structure and how does the future structure intertwine with the operational needs of the company?

- **Deal team**. Who are the people responsible for various parts of the deal, and what is their track record or history of success?

- **Post-closing operating plan and financials**. How does the operating plan to execute align with financial projections and models?

· **Returning capital and investor return profile**. How does capital get returned and over what time period will it be returned? What is the return profile investors may expect to receive?

WAYS TO FINANCE FOR GROWTH
Debt

Many company owners have mixed feelings about debt in their mind, but borrowing can be a very useful tool to finance for growth if leveraged correctly. Taking on debt allows a company to expend much more capital to grow without hurting profits in the short term. If leveraged correctly, the return seen from investing the funds gained from the debt will outweigh the interest expense accrued.

Let's take a manufacturing plant, for example. As that type of company is looking to change its production capacity, there will likely be a need for capital expenditure. Purchasing equipment, which is generally a highly leverageable asset, can make a good deal of sense as there is a lot of inexpensive debt available for many types of equipment that fit into a production line.

Taking on debt often allows an owner to maintain all of the equity they currently own in a company. The interest expense and principal of a loan for a borrower can be classified as a business expense and can therefore be deducted from a business's total income, reducing taxes paid.

There are drawbacks with debt, however; for instance, at some point, the money does have to be repaid. Therefore, it is important to understand the difference between short-term and long-term debt and the ever-important cash flows associated with deploying debt as a growth strategy. One of the biggest issues we see is when short-term debt is used for long-term assets, or when long-term debt is used to fund short-term operating losses.

Most founders and business owners might be very familiar with certain aspects of debt through other investments—perhaps in personal home mortgages or other real estate investments. There is a familiarity with how borrowing funds and paying them back works. However, a few aspects are quite different when it comes to utilizing debt at an institutional level. Whether from a bank or a credit fund, there tend to be substantial differences in how loans are structured, managed, and dealt with. We are not going to cover all of those in this book, but we do cover a few key points about debt that are sometimes missed.

Ratios. With debt, some common ratios apply, and it's important to be familiar with them. For instance, if you're buying your first home, a loan-to-value of 80 percent is a good rule of thumb. If you are buying a commercial property, a 65 to 70 percent loan-to-value is a good rule of thumb.

Companies do not have the exact metrics that exist in real estate, but there are some fairly good ones. Those ratios will hit on leverage ratios relative to EBITDA. Traditionally, we see a comfort level with pure founder-owned businesses that can receive 2x to 3x EBITDA on a loan. For example, a company doing $5 million of EBITDA, depending on the industry and lending conditions, can sometimes obtain $10 to $15 million of debt. If the company has an equity sponsor or third-party equity behind it, that number can rise to 3x to

4x. If it is a scaled company with scaled equity providers, that number can exceed 4x in leverage. Be sure to also have a good grasp on coverage ratios (some of the most common ratios can be found in the Appendices). Advance rates and debt service coverage ratios are two in particular to pay attention to.

Recourse versus nonrecourse. There are two types of debt that many business owners probably recognize, but they do not fully understand the flexibilities they can provide. A recourse debt holds a borrower personally liable, and their personal balance sheet solely supports the loan. Nonrecourse debt holders are not personally liable, and their company's balance sheet supports the loan.

As the name implies, in the event of liquidation, if there's still a balance remaining after the collateral is collected, recourse loans allow lenders to go after other assets owned by the borrower. Lenders of nonrecourse loans, on the other hand, are not in a position to go after a borrower's other assets even if there's an outstanding balance after the collateral is sold.

Recourse loans tend to require a fairly stringent failure guarantee. We will spend a little more time on nonrecourse loans and their variations, as they do not simply rely on the business owner for repayment of the loan. Many times, entrepreneurs and founders will say that most of their net worth is tied up in the company. This causes a personal risk if something happens to the company.

This difference becomes especially important to a founder if there is a problematic situation or an issue with a loan performing. The recourse loan allows the bank to have a perceived edge over the founder in negotiating terms and conditions versus a nonrecourse loan. A nonrecourse loan creates a psychological leveling ground, if you will, for negotiating under distressed conditions with regard to the bank. If there is too much pressure, the founder can literally hand over the keys and walk away without having to deal with some of the complexities of the business winding down. This is rare and definitely not a recommended strategy, but it is the founder's counterbalance to a less than fortunate performance scenario for the company and negotiations.

Interest rate swaps. An interest rate swap is a forward contract that determines that future interest payments will be based on a predetermined, specific principal amount. It is a derivative tool that is typically used to take a floating rate loan (a loan that moves up and down with either live or prime rates) and exchange it for a fixed-rate loan, or vice versa. It does so by utilizing a third party.

An interest rate swap can often add cost to a loan, but depending on the rate environment, it can be a huge value add as well. An interest rate swap acts as a derivative on top of the loan that stabilizes the rate that the borrower pays. So, even though the underlying rate goes up and down, the value of the swap moves in opposite directions with ups and downs in interest rate volatility, allowing the borrower to make known payments despite interest rate volatility.

Having some sort of interest rate hedge is usually a part of any sort of higher leverage use of more institutionalized capital. This is simply so bankers and other participants can look at a moment in time and understand that interest rates should not be able to ruin a favorable deal. The interest rates, if frozen, leave the performance of the business to determine positive or negative results rather than setting up a great deal, only to have it fall apart just because interest rates ticked up 300 basis points.

I am typically a proponent of interest rate swaps. Even though they may cost 50, 60, 75, or even more basis points (depending on the time frame and milestones, etc.), they are usually worth the cost relative to the predictability and the outcome of the underlying debt.

Cash-flow term loans. A cash-flow term loan is exactly what it sounds like: a loan based on past, present, and forecasted cash flow. A company can borrow based on expected revenues. A cash-flow term loan doesn't require physical company or personal assets to be leveraged as collateral. It typically has an amortization schedule over three, five, seven, or 10 years, but it may also include a component that involves a *cash-flow sweep*. For example, if a company needs to increase inventory for an upcoming typically high-selling season, it could utilize a cash-flow term loan, then pay the loan back with interest once the inventory sells.

A cash-flow sweep speeds up amortization (lowering the principal of a loan) if there is a level of targeted cash at the end of the year. If there is anything above that, a percentage of this may go back to the bank to further reduce and pay down the principal. Cash-flow sweeps are sometimes overlooked, despite initial documents and underwriting having planned for them. Cash-flow loans offer a welcome tool to have—in particular, for leveraged buyouts.

Joint venture

A joint venture is the combining of two otherwise unrelated companies in a common project in order to benefit from each other's expertise, resources, and access to new markets.

A joint venture offers several advantages to its participants by sharing:

1. **Investment and expenses.** Each company contributes a portion of the initial capital needed for the project, and may share a common pool of resources, which can bring down costs on an overall basis. For example, in many cases, each company involved could share accounting resources, team members, human resources, real estate, machinery, and so on.

2. **Technical expertise and know-how.** Each company brings its own specialized expertise and knowledge that can complement and strengthen each other's skills.

3. **Markets.** A joint venture may enable companies to enter each other's markets. For example, if a company headquartered in Region A enters into a joint agreement with a company headquartered in Region B, both companies can expand their product portfolio and market size.

4. **New revenue streams and other synergy benefits.** The goal of a joint venture is to create new revenue streams for both companies by creating a product or service that neither could exploit on their own. Financial synergy can lower the cost of capital, while operational synergy can increase operational efficiency.

5. **Intellectual property.** Companies often enter into joint ventures with technology-rich firms to gain access to such assets without having to spend the time and money needed to develop the assets for themselves. For example, in 2019, the Swedish automaker Volvo and ride-hailing firm Uber unveiled a jointly developed production car that was capable of driving by itself and represented the next step in the "strategic collaboration" between both companies. Volvo provided the cars, while Uber focused on the self-driving technology.

6. **Brand credibility.** Forming a joint venture with a larger, well-known brand can help a small company achieve enhanced marketplace visibility and credibility.

7. **Blocking the competition.** If two companies are already competing in the same market, a successful joint venture can effectively erect barriers that make it difficult for competitors to penetrate the marketplace.

8. **Gain institutional interest.** For companies that are not yet large enough in scale and revenue to generate interest from institutional investors, two or more entities can join forces to become more appealing to investors looking for larger-scale opportunities.

Yet even the best-intended joint ventures can go awry. The main risks of a joint venture include:

1. **Confusion.** This commonly happens in the absence of clear objectives. Pursuing separate objectives will threaten

the success of the venture. For this reason, the objectives of the venture need to be clearly defined and communicated to everyone involved at the outset. Always quantify objectives when possible, ensure alignment, and document everything.

2. **Cultural clashes and differing management styles.** This can be a big problem for JVs that look good on paper but become a nightmare in practice. For example, in 1999, Siemens of Germany and Fujitsu of Japan announced they would combine their European computer businesses. The new entity, with total annual revenue of more than $6 billion, would rank as the world's fifth-largest computer maker after Compaq, Dell Computer, IBM, and Hewlett-Packard. It lasted 10 years, until in 2009, when it was dissolved for what some analysts believed were reasons of persistent cultural incompatibility.[8]

3. **Product disagreements.** For example, while the Volvo-Uber joint venture proceeded nicely, an earlier JV between Volvo and the Japanese automaker Mitsubishi ended badly. The idea was to produce a car in the Netherlands, popularly known as NedCar, but then Volvo's parent firm, Ford Motor Co., decided not to use the Mitsubishi-made car platforms. The project was terminated.

....

8   Rene Hordijk, "Organizational and Cultural Clash at Fujitsu-Siemens," *Grin.com*, 2000, https://www.grin.com/document/96884.

4. **Imbalance**. A real or perceived mismatch in the levels of investment, expertise, or assets brought into the venture by the involved parties may create friction. One party may begin to feel that it is contributing more than its fair share of resources to the project and grow to resent the agreed-upon distribution of profits. Such issues can be avoided by transparent planning, clear communication, and frank discussions during the formation of the joint venture, so that each party knows what it needs to contribute and what it will receive in return.

Self-financing

Self-financing is exactly that—financing without engaging anyone outside the company and instead using personal finances from a company owner (or several owners) or the business's profits. This occurs when a profitable company foregoes the option of distributing profits and instead reinvests profits to grow the company. This option has many pros, including:

- Increases value of the businesses with no outside influence or costs
- Company owner(s) able to maintain control and not lose equity
- Improves a company's financial ratios, making it more attractive to outside investment
- Reduces a company's dependence on other financial backers
- Can reduce a company's level of debt very quickly

- Promotes the profitable business model that is in action
- Improves a company's credibility

Some of the downsides include:

- No (or less) profits are shared
- Amount invested is limited to the owner's (or owners') capital or to the company's profits
- Typically, a slower way to grow a company
- Exposes a company or individual's assets to any liability that it might incur

Perhaps the greatest example of growth through self-financing is Amazon.com. Since its founding in 1994, company head and biggest owner Jeff Bezos (today he owns 11 percent of the company's stock, making him the largest shareholder) pursued a strategy of no stock dividends, instead plowing every penny of profit back into the company. As Jason Del Ray wrote for Vox Media:

> . . . The company's promise to investors has instead been built around the idea that as Amazon grows, eats up business in new markets, and starts generating meaningful profit, investors will get more excited about buying the stock, pushing the price up.[9]

....

9   Jason Del Rey, "Walmart Paid Wall Street Investors $12 Billion Last Year to Keep Them Happy. Amazon Paid $0.", Vox, February 18, 2020, https://www.vox.com/recode/2020/2/18/21142153/amazon-walmart-dividend-stock-buyback-wall-street-investors.

Financial investors

Utilizing financial investors can allow a company to gain a large amount of capital to be used for any purpose, and it never has to be directly repaid. It can also allow a low-earning company to maneuver more freely due to the large infusion of cash that the company may receive.

The main downside of financial investors is that, by accepting the investment, the company takes on an additional partner who, depending on terms and conditions, is entitled to both a say in how the company is run as well as a portion of the profits.

If you watch *Shark Tank*, this is a conundrum that contestants frequently face. The tempting offer of capital is often accompanied with "In exchange, I want 30 percent of your company," or some such high percentage. The contestant pauses and says, "Will you take 20 percent?"

The danger is that once an outside investor takes an ownership chunk, then that chunk is no longer available; it's off the table. The most anyone can own of a company is 100 percent. Selling meaningful portions of a company should be well-thought-through so that the founder's time, capital needs, and desired ownership levels are congruent with each other.

Recapitalization

Recapitalization is restructuring a company's debt and/or equity mixture, often with the aim of making a company's capital structure more optimal from either a financial or stakeholder perspective. The process essentially involves raising one or more forms of capital to effect a meaningful change in the capitalization structure of the company.

Most recapitalizations fall into two simplified transactions of either debt being used to replace equity, or equity being used to replace debt. However, the subcategories of types of capital, structures, and strategies are quite diverse. A company's strategic needs and financial condition will typically shape the recapitalization options available to it. The main forms of recapitalization include:

"Chips" off the table

Diversification—When things are going well, it is wise to think about creating liquidity and diversification by taking a portion of a company's value out in cash via a special dividend. This is especially true for owners getting closer to retirement, who might have neither the time nor the desire to weather an economic downturn.

Estate planning—For owners who are not ready to sell, but would like to position their estates, fund foundations, fund a family office, or enact certain gifts, a recapitalization can create the cash in order to make this happen without selling the company. Also, for family-company scenarios, a recapitalization can be used to equalize the wealth of the children involved in the company (stock) and those that are not (cash).

Capital shift

Growth—For many companies, exciting growth requires capital. Looking toward a recapitalization for the purpose of reinvesting company-generated cash in growth strategies is a viable means to meet demand.

One company to another—For various reasons, an owner may want to shift capital from one company to another, and a recapitalization makes this possible.

Holding company dividend—For holding companies with various subsidiaries, recapitalizing a subsidiary can create capital that, in turn, can be given to the holding company in the form of a dividend, and that capital may be repurposed in various ways.

Buyout of an equity stakeholder

Divestiture or spin out—When a parent/sub or private equity relationship hasn't quite worked out according to plan or has run its time frame course, a recapitalization can provide the means to affect a management buyout.

Retirement/family transition—When there are three partners in a company with one retiring, a recapitalization can be used to buy out the retiring partners' shares using the company's financials instead of using the personal net worth of the other two owners.

Recapitalizations are especially effective in a family transition when the incoming generation needs to raise funds in order to acquire the shares of the outgoing generation.

Inactive shareholders—Whether it's one shareholder or many smaller shareholders, if the company is experiencing growth, it may be more efficient to recapitalize the company to buy back the shares of the inactive participants instead of letting the inactive shareholders reap the rewards of equity growth.

WHY RECAPITALIZE

There are plenty of reasons why a company's management team might want to buy out an existing owner or equity sponsor (PE firm or holding company) or consider a recapitalization. However, a common thread is that the seller and buyer have taken the perspective that cash in the hands of the seller is of greater importance than the seller's continued involvement in the company (typically for time frame, contribution, or philosophical reasons). Usually, the relationship with the equity sponsor has "run its course," and they seek liquidity, while management wants to retain equity control of the company. A recapitalization can accomplish these goals, giving the exiting partner their liquidity and keeping control in the hands of management.

Some other benefits of recapitalization include:

Allowing shareholder liquidity. A recapitalization allows for shareholders of different classes to obtain liquidity without an outright sale.

Reduce the financial burden. In this situation, the company will reduce the cost and cash flow burden by paying down debt with funds gained from selling equity.

Growth funding. A company can also utilize a recapitalization when a portion of the funds are used on the balance sheet to fund growth initiatives (primary capital) in addition to shareholder liquidity (secondary capital).

Reorganization during bankruptcy. Recapitalization expectations should be set by balancing the current or projected operating environment of the business, amount of capital required, and the company's ability to satisfy due diligence requirements. Companies and their owners may need to think through how a recapitalization may dilute current ownership.

It is important to note that planning in advance for a recapitalization is a key component of the process. On average, a successful recapitalization may take three to 12 months from engagement to closing.

THE FIVE CORE ELEMENTS OF A GROWTH STRATEGY

Growth strategies take several different forms, but over the course of a career, we have seen a consistent method that we feel is the core of all growth planning. We've utilized these strategies with several companies that have seen significant growth. While there may be subtle to significant adds based on the industry in which a company operates, the core elements are highly universal in how they are applied. This method of growth strategy planning generally has five core elements:

1. Marketing

Marketing is the fulfillment of the idea that there are higher-reaching activities that can be done to create opportunities for revenue. Marketing is sometimes confused with sales, but they are very different. Marketing is the overall positioning of the company in the market and the overall positioning of the brand it drives. There may be elements of marketing that drive customers to the brand itself, but marketing is not sales.

Marketing is the first step in getting leads interested, while sales takes that interest and converts it. Sales and marketing complement each other, and it is imperative that there be transparency between the two.

2. Sales

Creating a sales forecast and sales development program is instrumental to bringing in new clients. Like any department, there should be a defined leader, and that leader should have the support, tools, and resources to execute on the appropriate sales strategy.

There are four sub-points to building a sales forecast effectively:

1. Align the sales process with the customer buying process.

2. Define each stage of the sales process and track it accordingly.

3. Analyze the pipeline that has been created through the process.

4. Ensure the sales team is trained well, not only on process, but also on process tracking. There should be a good alignment of incentives for both process and process tracking.

Be mindful of your different sales partners.

For example, a *channel partner* is a company that partners with a manufacturer or producer in order to market and sell the manufacturer's products, services, or technologies. Channel partners may be distributors, vendors, retailers, consultants, systems integrators

(SI), technology deployment consultancies, value-added resellers (VARs), or other such organizations.

Channel partners can be both great supplements and complements for growth. They can provide instant access to customers, but they come at a cost. This cost is not only financial; it is usually paired with some level of intellectual capital, property sharing, or technology sharing.

If a company decides to go down the road of working with a channel partner, it is important that they do not become so dependent on the channel partner that the company can barely function without it. It's a bit of a double-edged sword in that the channel partner can provide instant access to revenue, but if the business becomes so dependent on the channel partner, there could be a tipping point of seeing diminishing returns from an enterprise value perspective. Though the company may be growing, the more dependent it becomes on its channel partner, the less shareholder value is actually being created relative to other growth options. While that is not always the case, it certainly can be. This is why every company requires its own unique assessment using the channel partner distribution strategies.

3. Technology

Technology can play a pivotal role in making sure that growth happens efficiently. It is important to utilize the efficiencies of technologies to reduce wasted time, lessen the amount of human touches (which increases scalability), and make the most of each operational efficiency. Again, this could mean many different things for different companies and different industries. A combination of either hardware or software can allow a company to utilize technology to grow more efficiently. For one company, it may be having state-of-the-art equipment, while for another company, it may be having state-of-the-art software developed in-house, outsourced, or both. In almost all cases, an "ERP" (enterprise resource planning) system for accounting and data management is mission-critical.

One of the questions to ask is, "Is there a piece of hardware or a piece of software that could create more efficiency and lower costs?" For most industries in today's environment, growth comes from not only adding employees, but also adding technological advancements to better help these employees and make them more effective. Many of these technology enablers are found in quality ERP systems, CRM systems, and industry-specific software. Generally speaking, when planning for technology, we've seen the benefits of companies selecting systems from among the largest in their industries. This is likely when a low-risk decision (utilizing a highly recognized offering) is the best decision.

4. Talent

One of the most important factors in a good growth strategy is talent. Attracting and retaining the right talent is essential to helping the business grow. Whether this is on the sales side, technology side, or marketing side, it is imperative to have the right people supporting the growth initiative.

It is important to regularly assess the specific needs for human capital and determine if they are permanent or temporary. If they are temporary, it is usually best to outsource to the best-suited provider of that temporary service. If the need is temporary marketing or branding for a specific project, for example, a specific marketing/branding agency might be the best choice to propel the project forward. For something like sales, this might be more of a position that should be hired and trained from within. Overall, everything revolves around people and having the right people in place is key to a good business.

It is important to have assessment points along the way. If somebody is in a role for only a short period of time, there should be checks and balances with the new hires along the way. New talent should be additive to company values, day-to-day operations, and the overall organization. Each new person coming onboard during growth should also go through some sort of cultural immersion. For the most part, as a company grows, the overall culture should not be ripped apart in different ways, though some company cultures might need some altering to effectively move forward. If that is the case, it is important that each new hire builds toward a new culture.

Removing certain people is also an important element of maintaining talent within a company. This might be done to get rid of stagnation and complacency and support energy and growth. The same thing should also be true of outsourced consultants and providers. The outsourced people who are coming in need to be additive to the direction of culture rather than being anti-culture. Sometimes a company might even bring in somebody who pushes the culture in a new direction, but as long as that direction is desirable, I would not consider that to be anti-culture. This scenario would be much better than having somebody who says everything is great when a company is missing on key performance metrics.

5. Finance

Many business owners and founders today underestimate the role and importance of what modern finance can do for a company, which commonly leads to adverse outcomes. Many have made the right investment but failed to include somebody who has deep knowledge in these areas and would have created millions of dollars of value—either by allowing for things to occur or by enhancing things that did occur.

Furthermore, in the modern age, finance should also be lending itself to business intelligence that better prepares marketing, sales data, information, and product analysis. Better business intelligence leads to higher operational efficiencies, capital management, cash flow management, and traditional finance objectives. This is sometimes tricky for business owners who struggle to make the appropriate investment in a CFO or business intelligence/ERP systems (data visualization tools, CRMs), and they may be "penny-wise and pound-foolish" with those decisions.

In conclusion, encapsulating these five elements into a strategy document is essential for helping the company navigate through different periods within its life cycle. It can also be a check-in point to see if the company is really hitting its metrics. If not, what needs to get adjusted? Are market dynamics changing? What internal operational items need to be fixed in order to better prepare the company for the next 12 months?

Utilizing these strategies, we've worked with companies on expanding facilities, entering new product segments, creating M&A strategies, entering new geographic markets, and more. They are the core elements that lenders, investors, and buyers look for when trying to understand and validate a growth plan.

Chapter 3

MERGERS AND ACQUISITIONS

A business seeking to expand will often consider merging with another company as equals, or acquiring a smaller company to "roll up" into itself.

Some companies are very aggressive in pursuit of growth by acquisition. In the 1980s, under the leadership of CEO Jack Welch, General Electric was the king of M&A. During his tenure as boss of GE from 1981 to 2001, Welch oversaw more than 600 roll-up acquisitions, reimagining the company into a massive and diverse global conglomerate that encompassed sectors ranging from entertainment (RCA) to financial services (GE Capital). During that time, GE increased its market value from $12 billion in 1981 to $410 billion in 2001.

More recently, we've watched leading cloud-based software and CRM leader Salesforce work toward completing seven acquisitions within 10-plus years—surpassing $26 billion in annual revenue for the 2022 fiscal year.

On the other hand, a business owner seeking an exit will often solicit either a merger or an acquisition by a larger company or investment group.

This chapter will explain M&As from both points of view—that of the seller and the buyer.

It sounds somewhat clichéd to talk about sellers needing to consider "strategic" versus "financial" buyers. However, many potential sellers struggle with this concept and tend to err on either the aggressive side (values that are not always substantiated) or the conservative side (feeling they have to squeeze the extra dollar of EBITDA in case it will improve value). This chapter is geared toward putting these myths to rest and helping sellers get to the core of what matters when considering a discussion with strategic and financial buyers. The three main points we will cover include an overview of a buyer, valuation drivers, and other issues to consider.

STRATEGIC BUYERS

Strategic buyers are often looking to make an acquisition that furthers their company's growth plans—allowing them to add a new offering to market to clients, buy up market share, buy up a vertical, or expand a geographic footprint. There is the possibility to realize revenue expansion by cross-pollinating client lists with offerings or benefiting from economies of scale on the expense side.

Because of this, strategic buyers can often model enhanced financial performance well beyond what the seller has projected for its own performance. That is why they are able to pay more than a typical financial buyer. The better the fit, the more often it results in the buyer being willing to pay a greater purchase price.

The other reason strategic buyers are usually able to pay a higher price for companies than financial buyers has to do with their scale, access to capital, and whether the company is publicly traded or has easier access to capital.

Lastly, the strategic buyer is buying the company to enhance their own operations, drive efficiency, or create revenue opportunities in addition to the possibility of furthering the company's brand and market positioning.

Valuation drivers

Communicating value drivers to a strategic buyer is one of the most important components to maximizing the value of an offer to purchase. While this seems obvious, it's not always easy because it sometimes implies variables on the buyer side that are unknown to the seller, such as the buyer's better ability to gain distribution, leverage other resources to drive incremental sales, or even combine part of the seller's company with an asset they already own to maximize the potential return. The buyer therefore will be able to "overlay" their financials over the seller's projections to determine an ultimate value.

Adjusted EBITDA

Whenever one is going through modeling and financials, it is important to show performance of a business in the most realistic manner. This may mean not only taking the actual financials, but also adjusting them for certain non-core, nonrecurring conditions that may have previously affected the business. When we go through these reports and projections, we will usually pull out interest, taxes, depreciation, and amortization, and we will also have a line for adjustments.

The most legitimate and common adjustments that one can have and benefit from are the following one-time adjustments:

- One-time loss or one-time expense item. These expenses are typically removed and can be adjusted back out again as long as they are not recurring in nature.

- Expenses that are ending, such as a lease, double-up on human capital roles, a marketing contract that is coming to an end, and so on. It is okay to cut the tail of these nonrecurring, ending expenses.

- Expenses that are nonrecurring and non-cure. These are typically expenses that a company has not historically had and will most likely not have again. These can include, for example, a special trip or entertainment event.

- Excess compensation. Owners may sometimes take compensation in various forms such as cash, consulting agreements, or distributions. When this is in the form of salary and bonus, it is legitimate to go back and adjust compensation norms to levels that reflect or are comparable to industry market rates. These adjustments are often made for a strategic sale or certain acquisition perspective.

Integration-adjusted EBITDA

It often makes sense to take things one step further by determining an integration-adjusted EBITDA with the assumption that certain functions that would typically be gobbled up by a big company would be absorbed by the strategic buyer. Generally speaking, these functions might include:

- Human resources—not just human capital, but also the fact that they will have a lower-cost health program or a slightly different benefits program. Sometimes these costs can go up, but on a comparable basis, they should go down.
- CFO or third-party finance expenses are typically removed.
- Other expenses in the finance area, which could be audited, would go away as well.

Operational items

Lastly, in preparing for a strategic buyer transaction, review all operational items such as sales, technology, office space, and vendors, and determine what services (if any) could be shared. Depending on the company, the acquisition strategy of the strategic buyer may be such that the acquisition results in having a shared sales team, a shared technology pool, or shared human resources. This will often eliminate unnecessary redundancies and reduce overhead and even eliminate the need for office space; in addition, the new business may have better pricing with certain vendors than the ones the target company is currently using.

It's important to be aware of these factors in advance and understand that if there is going to be a strategic acquisition, it will be necessary to further adjust EBITDA to accurately capture those items.

OTHER CONSIDERATIONS

Like many major decisions in life and business, there is often a delicate balance between considerations. Here are three things to consider when it is time to think about strategic versus financial buyers.

1. **Getting the highest price**. If the goal of the sales process is to exit at the highest multiple, a focus of the auction process should be figuring out the best way to appeal to strategic buyers (in addition to financial buyers) who will be able to overlay the greatest revenue expansion and/or cost reduction pro formas.

2. **Concluding a great deal for the company and employees**. If a great price is a must but the seller wants to "protect" employees, a strategic buyer whose overlay is more focused on revenue opportunities is the most likely candidate. However, the seller should realize that this may or may not be the highest offer price.

3. **Seller/CEO desires to stay with company post sale.**
   The opportunity for the seller/CEO to sell into a strategic purchase and stay on for another "phase" does exist. In certain circumstances, it may be desirable for the purchasing company to have the selling company's CEO take on broader leadership and responsibilities throughout the buyer's organization.

Integration equals value creation

Integrating culture, revenue drivers, operating efficiencies, and leadership is likely the most important aspect of any acquisition strategy. This is often where the best and worst of deals transpire. It can make a *good deal* great—and a *potentially great deal* blow up. Integration planning is the deepest organizational effort of any acquisition strategy. While acquisition and financing decisions often take place in the boardroom, the work of integration is borne by the staff and is very important to the success of the deal.

Management must sift through the following key topics:

- Product and service gaps and overlaps
- Distribution channel methods
- Operating functionality
- IT and enterprise systems
- Leadership and talent retention
- Capital structure optimization

ENTICING COMPANY OWNERS TO SELL

For a buy-side strategic approach, one of the tactics for explaining value to sellers is converting tax-equivalent income over certain time periods to equate to the cash compensation that an owner takes out of the business. One of the ways to show this is by expressing the value in terms of the number of years of income equivalency.

For example, imagine someone will receive net after tax $1.5 million for their shares of a company and is currently making $150,000 per year in salary after taxes. In this case, the sale would equate to 10 years of income. If you apply inflation, interest, and such, that number could push out to 12 or 13 years. This is important because even though $1.5 million may not sound like a lot to some, if it's expressed in terms of equating to 12 years' worth of work, it starts to hit home from a cash flow perspective. You can illustrate further how these proceeds from the sale can then be invested to receive a passive income in returns.

UNDERSTANDING TIMING

The use of time can be a tool used to appropriately acquire an asset. Based on the company, its different life cycle needs, etc., time can be your friend or your enemy. From a buyer's perspective, it's often gauged on the condition of the company.

Speed is quite important to a buyer when considering a high-growth company or a company that has attractive features. As a buyer, you want to acquire the company rather quickly to catch it at a lower valuation. If you wait too long, the company can get more and more expensive. As the seller in this scenario, time can be your friend and can be a way to show more value if you have a healthily growing business and a good environment for capital investment.

On the other hand, if a company is stagnant, contracting, or experiencing any instances of potential distress, more time becomes the friend of the buyer and the enemy of the seller. When a buyer knows there is a potential for a financial hiccup or concern, they will typically want to play a waiting game to see how the financial hiccup plays out. This can sometimes happen right as that financial hiccup is about to turn back into a good scenario. There is usually a window of time when the seller has been very long in the process and probably has some element of deal fatigue, making them more willing to accept certain values, terms, and conditions that, if they were in an otherwise more positive situation, they would not have accepted.

HIRING AN INVESTMENT BANKER

The role of the advisor or the investment banker in any sort of capital raising process, merger, or acquisition is to serve three essential functions:

1. **Preparation**—Company acquired, financial documentation in order, objectives aligned, and all team members prepared. This often includes financial materials and documents, financial models, marketing information, nondisclosure agreements, and confidential information memorandums set in place.

2. **Marketing/Deal Solicitation**—Marketing the business to various capital providers in an efficient way for management,

reducing management's time and increasing the probability of success.

3. **Guidance and Advisory**—Providing management guidance on selecting a financial partner and guiding the capital placement or merger and acquisition to close.

PREPARE EARLY

It may be prudent to start a discussion with an investment banker a year or two prior to an actual need for capital or desire to do a merger, acquisition, or disposition sale. As markets change and shift, or if management is so entrenched in figuring out and mastering their day-to-day, it is easy to miss or lose sight of some of the investing, acquisition, and valuation trends going on in the investment community.

It's important to get some of that information prior to when you know you'll need it and before the process begins. If you're considering a transaction of some kind, it's never too early to start shaping the company's direction toward efforts that will best serve its purpose for bringing in capital or completing a merger or acquisition. Some of those things may include shifting to a more industry-standard enterprise resource planning (ERP) system that would make an acquisition easier, integrating financials and operational information from one entity to another, having certain protocols changed or updated, putting certain systems in place, or placing more or less emphasis on certain types of customer contracts that will be beneficial for the transaction. All of these things, if given the appropriate amount of time, are important in better preparing for the success of a capital raise or a merger/acquisition.

Many times, these important tasks are left unchecked, and it's during the process that participants realize these steps could have—and should have—been taken in order to maximize value. By the time the process is already ongoing, it is too late. In this event, either value or timing suffer, meaning either the seller accepts a lower valuation or the buyer accepts a higher valuation. This is one area where having good advice *before* a capital raise or M&A transaction will typically put the company in a better position.

WHAT TO EXPECT FROM THE PROCESS

Typically, there will be three prongs of an engagement agreement: Terms and Conditions, Structure, and Other Subcomponents.

Terms and Conditions

There are typically certain terms and conditions of representation. Many investment banks and advisors require an exclusive contract, and this simply means that the company has the exclusive ability to represent the company for a period of time. There are usually terms and conditions around time frame of representation and what is called the *tail period*, which is when interested parties are brought to the table, but a transaction does not take place during this short window of representation. If a transaction does occur with one of those parties, that would still count for a fee. Several things are set up in an investment banking contract in order to present what is known as a *perverse incentive*. This is an incentive that has an unintended and undesirable result, contrary to the intentions of its designers.

This means that there is an actual incentive for the company to get inexpensive work done early, by using an investment bank to get investors, buyers, and sellers to the table, and then dismiss the investment bank. Many features in investment banking engagement letters are set up to simply prevent that perverse incentive from doing just that.

Structure

The next component is deal structure. These fee structures can be complicated and at other times quite simple, but there are essentially two primary components to most engagement agreements:

1. The first is a retainer. Most firms in today's marketplace charge a first-month retainer and an ongoing retainer.

2. The second is a success fee. Once a deal closes, there is a percentage of either capital or deal value.

Other Subcomponents

There are a variety of other issues that could affect the terms or structure of an engagement agreement. One could be marketing expenses that need to be accounted for, another could be expenses that are in addition to a success fee, and yet another could be an equity percentage of the company's earnings.

Elements of a smooth process

What makes a good investment banking process? There are almost too many things to mention, but a good process is typically hallmarked by having the following:

1. A high-quality teaser and an NDA that protects the company but does not offend capital providers

2. A CIM (confidential information memorandum) that professionally reflects the essential aspects of the company

3. Financial models that are realistic, well done, and present an accurate financial projection for the business going forward

4. Getting multiple offers, if possible, and presenting those to the client

5. Management meetings that are well-orchestrated and well-designed

These are some of the hallmarks of what you should expect from a financial advisor.

Investment bankers can also provide many post-transaction benefits. Some investment bankers, particularly if you are doing a roll-up strategy, have levels of operational experience that can be helpful in terms of guiding companies toward the ideal integration policy and are able to help a company navigate those waters in a way that builds value.

HOW TO SELECT AN INVESTMENT BANK

When selecting an investment bank or advisor, look for a personality match, a trust match, an attractive financial structure, and terms/conditions that are mutually acceptable. There should not be a clear winner or loser. If the company works too hard to negotiate a reduced fee, the investment bank may not work as hard or have as much incentive to do a good job. If the fee is too high, too complicated, or too egregious, the investment bank has taken advantage of the position of trust and has not done what they were supposed to do, at least in terms of a philosophical perspective.

When selecting a bank, it is important to ensure the bank has a general understanding of the industry's layout. Some of the large investment houses with investment banking divisions or practices include Goldman Sachs, Morgan Stanley, and Citi. There are also international investment-bank-only firms like Lazard. There are also regional investment banks that focus either on a particular region or on a particular vertical. For example, this might include a group that focuses on the Midwest, or a group that focuses on tech. These groups have some sort of focused effort and have somewhere between 40 and 1,000 employees.

Lastly, there are boutiques, which are typically either more regional or vertical focused. They usually have under 40 employees, and many even under 10. They look to develop, maintain, and build on the relationships they have. In most cases, a boutique investment bank is more prolific in certain geographic areas where there is a lack of larger investment banks. Boutique investment banks often exist in areas where having access to knowledge and good advice is viewed as a positive.

TYPES OF PROCESSES

When seeking to do a capital raise or a sell-side M&A project, companies can use a number of approaches, as described below.

The long-term play

The long-term play is where a company has identified early on a handful of potential investors and/or buyers, and there is a fairly transparent understanding that the parties over time will stay in touch and entertain doing future deals together. Many companies think this is the way things will ultimately go, and it is definitely a strategy to think about, though it does not necessarily lead to the best deal because it involves a fairly limited market and garners a fairly limited reaction.

Hide-and-seek method

In this strategy, a company may want to raise some capital or to sell but is doing so only under certain conditions and wants to get a feel for it from a select group of funds or strategic acquirers. The hide-and-seek is more of a casual reach out, typically through a third party, such as a financial intermediary or investment bank, that operates on behalf of the company. The company might express a mild interest in having some discussions, or allude to the fact that they are aware of someone or some company that could have interest in the space.

Just to gauge reaction, it is commonly good to go through this process in advance of running a full process to test the waters. Keep in mind, though, that this rarely results in an actual deal. It is more of a "what you give is what you get"; if you are giving faint signs of wanting to do something, you usually get faint signs of getting something in return. For that reason, this strategy is not often as productive as other approaches, but it has its place.

Limited strategic auction

With the limited strategic auction, a company says there exists a limited universe of people they would want to go into a deal with at this point in time. They provide full materials and full transparency, there is a desire to get a deal done, and the deal is taken from there.

General limited auction

A general limited auction includes a wider group of both strategic and financial buyers. These buyers may be more focused on a particular vertical, or there may be some element of strategic nature to the reason for the reach out. Maybe it is a company that would be a good add-on for a portfolio company of a private equity group, or it could be a good acquisition for a strategic buyer to further grow market share. It is a very transparent process that is open only to a select group larger than a limited strategic group, which is focused on strategic buyers only, but smaller than a full auction.

Full auction

A full auction means going to a very wide array of parties with the goal of attracting multiple offers. Those offers largely range in purpose and may be strategic or financial in nature. There may be a private equity group that wants to further deploy capital into a platform to grow it both organically and inorganically. There may be offers to buy the company as a tuck-in or an add-on to an existing company. Or there may be an offer from a buyer when the company could be a platform company. Overall, a full auction deal often includes a wide variety of different interests, different opportunities, different structures, and different viewpoints.

THE AUCTION PROCESS FLOW

To set the stage for an auction, the seller needs to produce a well-defined set of documents, including:

Investment summary—A brief overview of how the seller company would be an excellent investment opportunity.

Company overview—A short list and extrapolation of the key reasons why the company is worth acquiring.

Market analysis—Describes the market in which the seller operates and the seller's niche within that market.

Products and services—Describe the key products and services offered by the seller, as well as their margins. This can also include a list of significant customers and distribution channels.

Management—Provides an overview of the management team and the qualifications of those managers expected to transfer to the buyer.

Historical and forecasted financial statements—Include audited financial statements (without footnotes) for at least the past two years (and preferably more). They should also include an estimate of future financial performance for at least the current and following year.

Capitalization table—Summarizes investor ownership by class of stock.

Concluding remarks—A summary of the investment proposition with highlights from preceding sections.

ROLL-UP ACQUISITIONS

A *roll-up* generally occurs when smaller companies that operate in a similar fragmented industry or market are acquired and merged together either under or into a larger "platform" company. Although we spend more time describing this process, its elements can be applied to many of the previous processes. From the point of view of the buyer, the primary objectives of a roll-up are to:

· Increase revenue through incentives (earn-outs to the seller/pricing advantages/cross-selling)

· Reduce costs through operating efficiencies

· Increase the value of the company through both scale and diversity of EBITDA

A roll-up can speed up the building of a company or of a company's end goals when it would take too much time and capital to create a similar outcome organically. A roll-up often includes an exit goal either to make an acquisition of the overall company as attractive as possible for a larger organization or to complete an IPO. The following chart highlights the valuation objective of a successfully executed roll-up growth strategy.

Example Value Path
(Multiple of EBITDA)

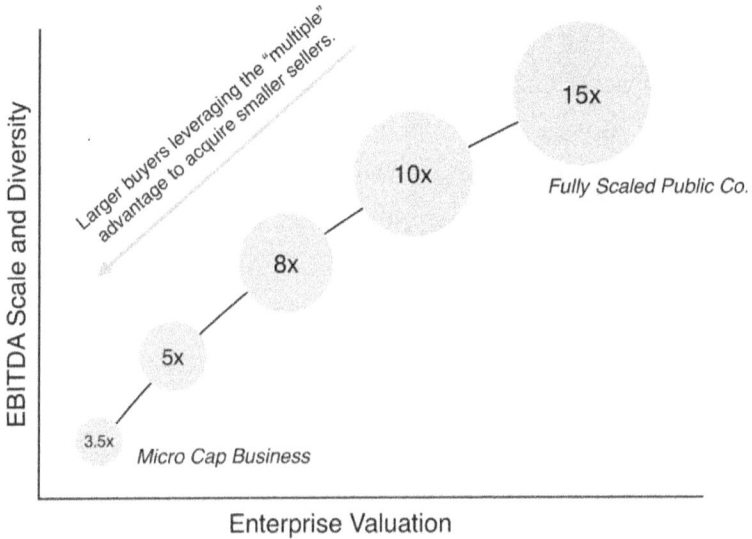

Larger buyers leveraging the "multiple" advantage to acquire smaller sellers.

15x

Fully Scaled Public Co.

10x

8x

5x

3.5x Micro Cap Business

EBITDA Scale and Diversity

Enterprise Valuation

Developing a plan and goals for a roll-up

A well-thought-out roll-up plan establishes a method for target selection, valuation, acquisition, and the eventual integration of two or more companies. While this may sound overwhelming, it's imperative to establish a specific goal that the roll-up should fulfill and construct a plan and strategy around it. A goal could be anything from expanding a company's geographic footprint to rolling up several businesses in an industry in order to capitalize on the economies of scale. Whatever the goal may be, it is extremely essential to keep the goal in focus because it is easy to get distracted and look for value in the wrong places.

After a specific goal for a roll-up has been established and several target companies that satisfy the main goal have been identified, the next move is to create a purchase strategy. A purchase strategy is how a company will finance a roll-up. Although most businesses want to see cash when selling out, it is possible to finance a deal completely through equity. A more common strategy involves using a private equity firm to help fund part of the deal in exchange for equity. In almost every scenario, the resulting entity will have taken on some form of debt in order to finance the deal. This is extremely common for these types of transactions, and if executed correctly, it can rapidly increase the value of a firm without greatly impacting the cash flow of a business.

Roll-up synergies

When combining different companies in a roll-up, it is important to look for synergies or the ability to create synergies at different levels. For example:

1) Customer overlap

Customer overlap is usually the easiest to recognize. This overlap may result from two of the target companies being competitors. That being said, do not just mash together two customer lists on paper and cross-sell. It is important to understand the sales, marketing, adoption, and use of the company relative to the acquisition. We have been in a situation where we thought there were going to be customer synergies, but the two products had completely different buying behaviors. If there is too much of a misalignment between a product or service, using marketing and sales can lead to disappointing results as the processes may not translate very well.

2) Service capabilities

A roll-up can create service capabilities. This can be exciting, especially when there is a new product or service capability that is one or two degrees different than what the acquiring company currently has. They don't need to be completely different, but different enough to be better together versus separately.

This is where the magic of combining two companies comes into play. Take, for example, two food services companies combining, such as a dairy and a meat company, into a new kind of company that can distribute both. If the capabilities are not too different, it can allow for various synergies to occur, particularly in the areas of customer overlap. For example, both of these need to be refrigerated, both should have teams in place that are accustomed to handling proteins, and so on.

So, for a food service company that has traditionally provided meat products to grocery and now provides dairy, it is fairly likely that that crossover could occur—in operations, distribution, sales and marketing, and so on. Given that they are both selling into grocery, some levels of marketing and sales may be able to have shared services or easier transitions to cross-selling different products and services to the same customers.

3) Operational synergies

If the businesses overlap so much that there is not a new product offering or a new real opportunity for cross-selling customers, there is an opportunity to consolidate the back offices. This is one of the most fairly common integrations following an acquisition, particularly in traditional businesses, such as financial service companies, accounting firms, and other businesses with highly replicable transactions, products, or services being offered.

In an ideal world, from a high-level mapping perspective, there will be both revenue/expense synergies and capability expansion. Transactions that involve operational synergies generally have a lower risk factor given that they rely less on consumer/customer behavior compared to other types of businesses. Relying on consumer behaviors brings a higher level of variables and subjectivity and often means that a business has to make a fair amount of assumptions in the planning process that may be false.

The importance of due diligence

A well-executed integration plan relies heavily on thorough diligence efforts leading to a possible merger. This initial diligence up front is done to make sure that personnel, statistic usage per unit, and employee items and leases can be legitimately combined.

For instance, let's say a customer assistance group can comfortably handle up to 100 customers a day per customer service employee. It would be a mistake to go into planning and assume that that number could be increased to up to 150 customers per customer service employee. This could lead to customer frustration, brand deterioration, and ultimately revenue loss.

It is exceptionally important to make sure that the understandings and diligence look good not only on paper, but also that the metrics make sense from an operating perspective. Otherwise, you could be pushing two companies together and realizing only a fraction of the synergies. Unfortunately, these lessons are sometimes only learned after a disaster has occurred because of poor planning, poor diligence, and poor understanding of what the businesses actually need to operate once they are combined into one.

Other roll-up items to consider

Integration

There are several other aspects to consider when targeting a business for acquisition. One is the possible ease or difficulty of integrating the two companies. While the financials may all work out, there still are times when the integration of another company can become complicated. A few examples of this include:

- Geographic—for example, travel distance or operating in different time zones

- Having competed with each other in the past

- Having fundamentally different cultures

- Disrupting long-standing procedures at one or both of the companies

All of these conflicts pose their own unique problems that a company must be prepared to remedy.

Eliminate redundant costs

Another aspect of a roll-up is eliminating redundant costs. For companies that are being rolled up within the same industry, there are often many ways to reduce costs. Common costs that can be centralized are shipping and freight costs, accounting, and the C-suite. For example, in manufacturing, costs typically drop due to economies of scale.

One of the larger dilemmas people face when performing a roll-up is which members of each company's C-suite to keep on, given the likelihood of redundant roles and capabilities. The C-suite is often the easiest place to reduce costs. However, this can be a precarious route. If the wrong people go, it can cause a slow in operations, or cause other people to leave the company as well, creating conflicts between new coworkers.

Matching goals with strategy

With the recent surge in private equity funding, the market has become quite crowded. New strategies, such as roll-ups, are needed to maintain large returns. Since roll-ups have become more popular, there are many people who have jumped into one without the proper planning and have seen their investments struggle, or even fail entirely. Moving steadily through this process is best, as it allows companies time to fully integrate and work out any issues that arise.

This is one of the keys to creating a profitable, lasting entity. Once an acquisition has been completed, a company may go about setting up a codified integration procedure to quicken the process during the next acquisition. In all, the major keys to successfully performing a roll-up are the following:

- Identify your ultimate goal and why it will be successful.

- Create a targeting strategy that synergizes with your goal.

- Move slowly in order to catch any issues or mistakes before they cause the whole operation to suffer.

LEVERAGED BUYOUTS

The advent of leveraged buyouts (LBOs) has brought about significant changes in U.S. acquisitions and divestitures. Understanding the transactions and their potential risk/reward trade-offs can help capital providers create markets and opportunities that didn't exist before.

In the 1970s, the leveraged buyout created a way for companies to be bought or sold using a combination of debt and equity. This combination fundamentally changed the U.S. mergers and acquisitions marketplace. Firms like Kohlberg Kravitz and Roberts (KKR) reinvented M&A by realizing that, in corporate America, many organizations had either over-diversified business lines, had expensive corporate overhead, or simply had poor management. They saw that the parts (divisions, business units, or assets) of companies were often worth more than the whole.

But this was just the first step. Having the necessary capital to acquire and unlock value was the next step. Buyout firms realized how a relatively small equity infusion and various forms of debt could be used to make the acquisitions. Thus, the term *hostile takeover* would take on new meaning as these transactions took off with popularity.

Many early LBOs consisted of the buyout firm simply acquiring the target organization and dismantling it as fast as it could. One of the primary reasons these short-term strategy transactions occurred was that in the early structures where senior banks played the primary capital role, loan amortizations and maturities were short-term in nature. Thus, using leverage was possible, but in general it was geared toward acquiring to dismantle versus acquiring to add value. It was during this time period that the "corporate raider" moniker was born, and films like *Wall Street* revealed what was going on in these deals.

That said, not all LBOs were corporate raider-type transactions; many deals during this period were value-add transactions. As the first decade of LBOs was drawing to a close, the largest LBO to date was completed: the RJR Nabisco acquisition by KKR for $25.42 billion (worth $61.73 billion in 2022 when adjusted for inflation) on October 24, 1988.[10] This amount was almost double the value of the $13.4 billion takeover of Gulf Corp., just four years earlier.

....

10 Rick Gladstone, "Kohlberg Kravis Wins RJR Nabisco With Blockbuster $24.53 Billion Bid," *AP News,* December 1, 1988, https://apnews.com/article/7eaf6313077bae6d1bc7ebdc8103 23e2. Source for inflation adjustment: https://www.usinflationcalculator.com/.

While these deals continued into the 1990s, drastic changes were underfoot in the capital markets. As interest rates declined, banks had more experience with these types of deals, private equity gained momentum, and mezzanine capital was born. The technology and equity market boom put fuel to the fire. In 1999, the total deal volume of LBOs was approximately $39 billion, but by 2007, the volume had ballooned to $518 billion for the year.[11] Growth was occurring at unprecedented rates.

In addition, the nature of the transaction was changing. While the 1980s were more about acquisition to dismantle, the 1990s brought about a new mentality of acquisition to grow and resell within three to seven years post-closing. The 1990s laid the groundwork for the next decade, which would see new heights in the use of LBO-structured transactions.

By 2000, the secret was out: LBOs had fantastic results, banks were lending money, mezzanine capital was available, and private equity was all the rage—so much so that even commercial banks wanted in, with more than just senior debt. They, too, wanted to dip down on the subordination rung with the goal of getting superior risk-adjusted returns. Banks did this through investments in mezzanine funds such as small business investment company (SBIC)

....

11 "Private Equity Spotlight—February 2008," *Prequin*, February 1, 2008, 5, https://www.preqin.com/insights/research/reports/private-equity-spotlight-february-2008. See also Roland Cornelius Südhof, "Leveraged Buyouts from 1999 to 2009: Is Bigger Really Better?," *scribd*, May 1, 2010, 4, https://www.scribd.com/document/32264014/LBOs-From-1999-to-2009.

funds, which attracted multiple bank investors and provided debt that was subordinate to typical senior credit facilities.[12]

With senior lenders having comfort, mezzanine capital available, and private equity flourishing, the first decade of the 2000s gave way to an LBO boom. Nine of the top 10 largest LBO deals of all time occurred in this third decade of the LBO. In terms of total deal value, global historical LBO activity has been present in $3.6 trillion of transactions from 1970 to 2007; however, 75 percent of that took place from 2001 to 2007.[13] History points us to trends, and if the trends are correct, we will continue to see LBOs play a significant role in corporate financial transactions, as evidenced by Elon Musk's 2022 acquisition of Twitter, which was one of the largest LBOs ever.

Today's LBO Marketplace

The marketplace for LBOs is robust for companies of all sizes, from mom and pop acquisitions using SBA financing to large and sophisticated transactions occurring in the public markets.

There are several reasons why LBOs play a major role in the U.S. and world economic growth and recovery, such as:

....

12 Scott Suttell, "Mezzanine Fund Finds Its Niche Paying Off," December 23, 1996, *Crain's Cleveland Business*, https://www.proquest.com/docview/198571687.

13 João Pinto, "The Economics of LBOs: Evidence from the Syndicated Loan Market," December 2021, https://www.researchgate.net/publication/356893556_The_Economics_of_LBOs_Evidence_from_the_Syndicated_Loan_Market.

Parts worth more than the whole. The 1980s-style corporate raider-type transactions may come back in vogue. Unlocking the value of smaller business units inside medium to large organizations may present opportunities as boards of directors are forced to obtain value for shareholders.

Management buyouts/succession planning. As the baby boomer generation ages, there has been and will be a need for those boomers who founded companies to obtain liquidity from illiquid businesses. This process perpetuates an LBO need as owners may not have sufficient capital to complete 100 percent equity-financed deals.

Private Equity Transactions. The thousands of private equity funds that exist today are all largely using some form of an LBO to complete their transactions.

LBO: strategy

The strategy of LBOs from a high-level perspective is fairly straightforward. Generally, there is a buyer who believes with high conviction that a target company will succeed in greater financial scale, and in a shorter time frame, than under current ownership and capital structure. The seller, on the other hand, generally desires to unlock value from the business or business unit and redeploy efforts or capital into other ventures.

The reason LBOs are so attractive is that they allow for transactions to occur on a fairly short timeline relative to the capital-intense nature of a pure equity acquisition. More importantly, in most cases they allow the buyer an opportunity to access needed capital without giving up a majority position in the equity of the company. This last factor is of critical importance.

Take, for instance, a business unit that is being bought out by a current management team of 10 people for $100 million. Assuming they have the ability to raise $5 million between the 10 managers, they would still be $95 million short. Taking the time to raise the remaining $95 million would be difficult, time-consuming, and may not lead to success. Alternatively, the availability of several layers of debt on top of the management team's $5 million of equity has possibilities.

Assuming that both efforts of raising $95 million of debt or $95 million of equity were equal, in terms of time frame and probability of success, from which one would the management team benefit more?

The answer to that question is found in the simple example below of a strategy to acquire to grow and sell. The end result is a significant windfall to the management team and provides them with $190 million more of net sale proceeds for essentially doing similar tasks. One could even argue that raising $100 million of equity is more difficult than $5 million of equity and $95 million of debt.

100% Equity Capital Scenario

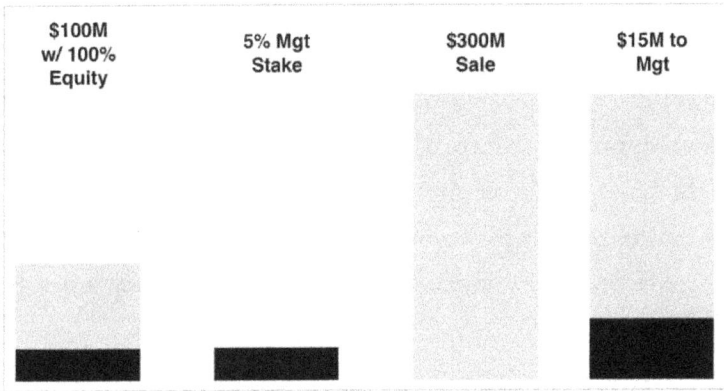

95% Debt and 5% Equity Capital Scenario

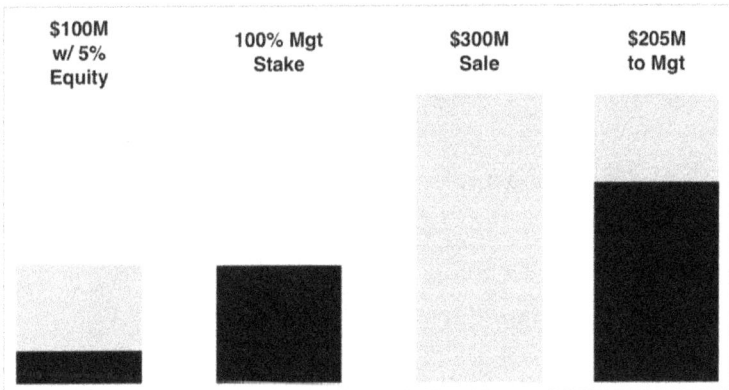

Comparison of All Equity and Equity/Debt Mix

The pure economics of LBOs are attractive to equity holders, but they also allow the equity holders to move quickly. Most deals do not sit around for long, especially if they are good ones. The LBO not only allows for the necessary capital, but also for quick action when action is the right course.

The following factors are recognized as the key drivers for a successful LBO:

Strong and stable free cash flow. This helps with the repayment of debt in the LBO structure.

Leading market position, brand, or clearly defined market niche. Market leadership increases the long-term stability and viability of the company.

Low capital-expenditure requirements. Low ongoing capital requirements allow for more free cash flow.

Low working-capital requirements. These requirements allow for more free cash flow without additional borrowing.

Good historical track record. Predictability of results is key.

Opportunity for margin improvement. Increasing revenue, decreasing expenses, or both can create more free cash flow.

Proven management. The ability to lead the company, especially through the strain of debt created in the LBO, is critical.

Further acquisition opportunities. The company may be a platform for other acquisitions or consolidations.

Possibilities for exit. Viability of an exit via IPO or sale may drive many of the fundamentals of the LBO.

The paramount goal in the LBO strategy is the creation of free cash flow to reduce debt and create shareholder equity value.

LBO: structure

Organizing a healthy deal structure is a balancing act between having the offer be attractive enough to a seller, but also balanced enough to meet the buyer's mid- and long-term objectives. While certain verticals may call for a simplistic structure, others may call for a relatively complex multiyear structure. Regardless of the complexity, having a format that fits into the company's culture is a key success factor in all acquisition-related activity.

The theory of LBOs is that a combination of debt and equity matched up with cash flows, tax benefits, and operational improvements can produce the ultimate deal structure. Getting this combination correct is what makes the difference between a deal that goes well and one that does not. The magnification of the use of leverage can create stellar returns.

There are three primary types of capital players in the LBO deal. Each player brings a different level of capital resource, return, and risk profile to the table. This powerful combination allows companies the ability to create significant value for both their own firms and capital providers.

Senior credit. This is typically provided by commercial banks. The types of credit provided tend to span the spectrum from short-term revolvers, to medium-term notes, to longer amortization balloon notes. Insurance companies provide longer-term amortizing senior debt as well. Usually, all senior LBO debt has the characteristic of amortizing principal over six months to seven years, with interest payments.

Mezzanine capital. Typically provided by mezzanine funds, private equity funds, or finance companies, this portion of the capital structure often consists of interest-only debt or long-term principal amortizations. In addition, the debt is subordinated to that of the senior debt, and therefore carries a higher interest rate. Mezzanine financing can often go hand in hand with warrants, or what is called an equity kicker. This adds return to the mezzanine investor's capital investment and compensates them for the risk of the subordination and interest-only structure.

Equity capital. This can come in two forms: preferred equity and common equity. The preferred equity typically carries a dividend rate and may have additional warrants attached to it. Common equity may also have two subclasses of voting and nonvoting shares. Equity is the final rung of capital subordination, providing the greatest return on capital, but also the highest risk level.

Generally speaking, the organization of capital is "tranched" between the primary capital providers and, in many cases, is further layered into different sections and types of debt and equity even within the primary category. Depending on the deal structure, the senior debt tranche of capital will range from 40 percent to 60 percent of the total capital structure, subordinated debt will range from 20 percent to 35 percent, and equity will range from 5 percent to 40 percent.

The following chart provides an example of how the capital structuring may look.

Capital organization plays a critical role in the return that equity sponsors achieve and also in the security that lenders have along the debt chain. The right capital structure can create value for all parties and allow for the deal to work based on the financial cash flow models.

Capital Organization

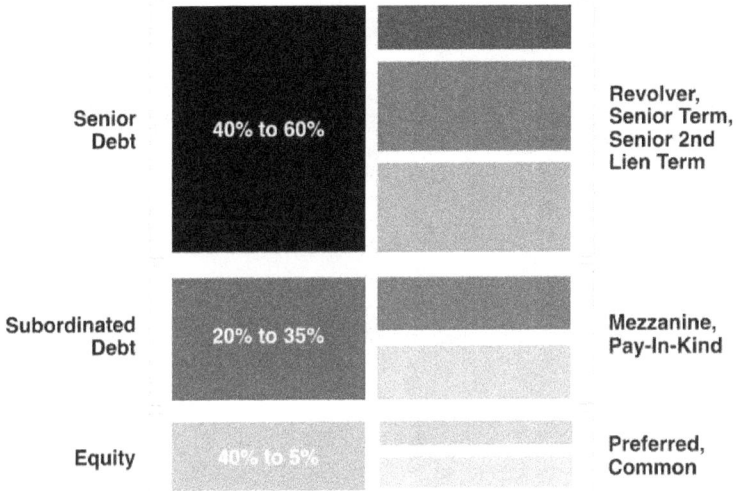

Senior Debt	40% to 60%	Revolver, Senior Term, Senior 2nd Lien Term
Subordinated Debt	20% to 35%	Mezzanine, Pay-In-Kind
Equity	40% to 5%	Preferred, Common

LBO: cash flow

The capital structure of the LBO is typically reverse-engineered based on the deal's historic, current, and future cash flows. The modeling of these cash flow scenarios is critical to the structuring of the LBO transaction. In general, capital providers want to ensure that cash flows are ample enough to meet the needs of debt service with a certain degree of financial cushion. The following chart details the commitment of cash flows to the capital structure. In general, a cushion of anywhere from 10 percent to 50 percent may be desirable based on the business, the deal structure, the total deal size, and other risk factors considered.

Cash Flow Priority Example

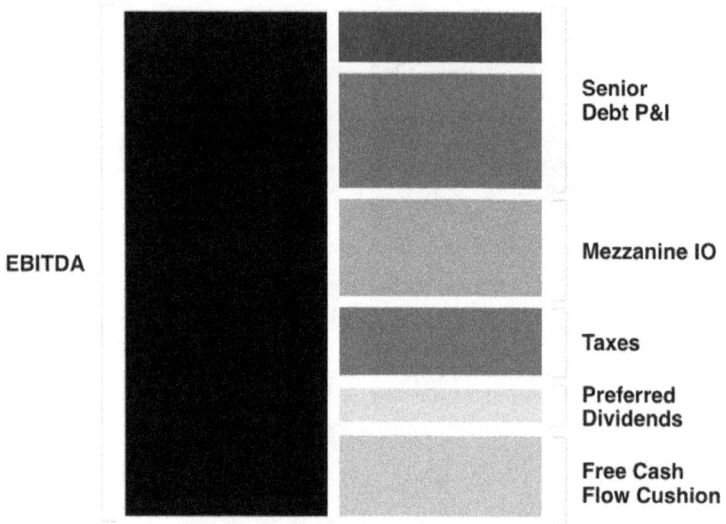

EBITDA

Senior
Debt P&I

Mezzanine IO

Taxes

Preferred
Dividends

Free Cash
Flow Cushion

Since the LBO is primarily a cash flow-lending transaction, the primary focus of the lenders and capital providers should be on the cash flow stability of the organization. They should ensure the created structure will be supported based on historical and projected future cash flows. After all, assets inside of the target company will usually provide little collateral or liquidation value. The primary asset in an LBO is the free cash flow created from business operations.

LBO: roles

Each player in an LBO has a certain role.

The commercial bank's role in the LBO process is to keenly understand the deal at hand and assess if the macro factors, business, management team, and the numbers will allow the bank to make a sound loan to the company. Like any transaction, understanding the risks and rewards are critical, but maybe more so for senior credit providers that participate in an LBO.

The role of senior credit in the LBO process is to provide base liquidity and the lion's share of capital needed to make the buyer's purchase from the seller possible. Banking regulators have published the *Leveraged Lending Comptroller's Handbook,* which states that when a bank is underwriting these types of LBO senior credits, the following critical issues should be addressed:[14]

- Appropriate loan structures

- Amortization requirements of term loans

- Collateral requirements, including acceptable types of collateral, loan to value limits, collateral margins, and appropriate valuation methodologies

- Covenant requirements, particularly minimum interest and fixed charge coverage and maximum leverage ratios

- How enterprise values and other intangible business values may be used, along with acceptable methodologies and frequency and independence of assessment reviews

. . . .

14 Office of the Comptroller of the Currency, "Leveraged Lending," *Comptroller's Handbook,* February 2008, https://occ.gov/publications-and-resources/publications/comptrollers-handbook/files/leveraged-lending/index-leveraged-lending.html.

- Minimum documentation requirements for appraisals and valuations, including enterprise values and other intangibles

- Acceptable fixed charge coverage ratios that reflect a borrower's ability to repay debt without undue reliance on refinancing

- For loans originated for sales, the degree to which underwriting standards are permitted by policy to deviate from underwriting standards for loans originated for portfolio or investment

- Banks that are lending in a senior credit capacity to LBOs should have these policies in place to ensure that lending activities are of a safe and sound nature

LBO: financial modeling

In financial modeling, the capital providers will want to understand the presented financial pro-formas and understand the detail and assumptions behind the models. The capital providers also run their own models that stress the financial performance of the company and gauge the key factors that could affect the company's ability to repay interest and principal and create compelling equity returns.

This is done primarily for senior credit, but the total credit obligation should also be assessed to see if different levels of the structure may have difficulty with repayment. The company may be acceptable with senior payments, but if subordinated payments run into difficulty, it may create other ancillary operating issues for the company, particularly if the subordinated lender or preferred shareholders have additional covenants, restrictions, or requirements.

Capital providers typically maintain ongoing financial models that provide insight into these key questions.

In the next section, a case study describes how many of these financial models are used to demonstrate the applicability of the financials to answer these questions.

LBO: bank terms, conditions, and covenants

When submitting terms for a specific transaction, lenders typically consider normal lending requirements. The terms, conditions, and covenants are on par with many other forms of lending; however, in larger-scale lending, personal guarantees from the borrowers are not in play. Therefore, the lenders are truly underwriting and preparing terms, conditions, and covenants to specifically match up to the specific deal. An example of abbreviated terms, conditions, and covenants for a hypothetical revolver for an LBO is detailed below:

Borrower—ABC Manufacturing

Business—Light manufacturer of a brand-name specialty product distributed via Home Depot and Lowe's on a national basis

Facility description—$100 million revolving line of credit due within 36 months

Pricing—Three-Month SOFR + 300 basis points, adjusting quarterly

Repayment—Interest payments due monthly

Purpose—Most senior form of debt in a $200 million LBO

Primary repayment—Operating cash flow

Secondary repayment—Restricted cash and cash equivalents of the corporation, as of the date of this term sheet valued at $25 million

Collateral—All business assets

Covenants—Interest and principal payments are senior to all other debt

Approval for common or preferred equity distributions

Approval for compensation increases for management and staff

Quarterly audited financials to be provided to lender

LBO: letter of intent

A sample letter of intent (LOI) can be found in the back of this book, but in general, the letter of intent is a nonbinding indication of certain aspects of a transaction that both parties mutually agree to work toward with their best effort and good faith. It is important to get this part right in the process, because at this point, a real relationship is being forged, whether it is a banking term sheet for senior debt growth equity or an ultimate M&A transaction.

This document serves as a reference to the final purchase agreement and as a guidepost to spell out the conditions under which the transaction would move forward. A letter of intent is a nonbinding document that has only one component—the exclusivity. Usually, in exchange for the buyer putting in the time to talk through diligence and assess the seller or the target company, they are given a period of exclusivity during which to complete their diligence.

Four key components are often found in a letter of intent that a company would put forward:

1. **Reasoning**. This is usually in the opening paragraph. There is some sort of cover letter or opening to the document that stresses certain reasons why the capital provider feels like it is a good fit for the company. It is usually good to keep this brief and restate a handful of key points as to why there is a good fit.

2. **Methodology**. This is more relevant to equity-related deals and M&A-related deals. The methodology of a buyer's valuation should be explained. This can be just a paragraph, but it usually covers the thought process of the valuation and what that valuation is.

3. **Capital**. For a growth-equity round or mezzanine round, this covers the amount of capital and may also cover the terms and conditions of the capital. If it is an M&A event, this could also be a spot where sources and uses are discussed. This middle piece is really where a lot of the meat of the LOI comes out.

4. **Additional items**. This may include the due diligence process or other unique aspects of a deal. It also might be included in the ladder section along with the process to get from an LOI to close.

By having these four components, there is a fairly clear road map as to why the companies should be working together and under what framework structure and capital levels they should work. It also explains how the parties would actually go from signing the LOI to an eventual close and any sort of additional terms and conditions that may be part of that process.

LBO: tax advantages

There are several tax advantages to leveraged buyouts, which can be a good and attractive vehicle.

The first is interest deductibility. Leveraged buyouts imply the use of leverage, and the interest is deductible under current tax law, reducing the financial impact or tax rate by a significant amount. This advantage is a significant way to utilize earnings to inexpensively bring in capital and then be able to deduct that cost.

The second major tax advantage is that existing shareholders are typically allowed to roll over ownership percentages into the new entity without a tax impact. So even though a transaction has occurred, it usually can be structured so there is neither a financial tie nor a tax consequence to a seller who rolls over a percentage of their shares.

The third advantage is inexpensive stock grants. This is due to leverage that compresses the equity value of the company and allows the company to grant shares of stock on an inexpensive basis. As the company grows, not only will the equity increase, but as the debt is repaid and principal is reduced, it will further increase equity value. The two-pronged approach depresses the asset value at the time of grant, which becomes worth a substantial amount in three to five years as the company grows and debt is repaid.

The other tax advantage of an LBO is a step-up in cost basis in the stock, so that the acquirer has an increased basis at the point when they are eventually sold.

Finally, the fourth advantage is depreciation. Depending on how the transaction is structured, depreciation can be factored in to help further reduce tax liabilities and increase cash flow to the company. An example is depreciating certain assets (physical assets and/or goodwill) over a period of perhaps 15 years.

LBO: acquisition strategy

Planning specific goals for a strategy of growth through acquisition is of key importance. As part of the planning process, it's important that several target companies that satisfy the main goal can be identified. Relying on too few opportunities can reduce the odds of success, while a "target-rich environment" can aid in success.

It's also important to understand what acquisition structure will meet the balanced needs of getting a seller to sell and creating accretive value for the buyer.

Lastly, acquisition integration planning can never be underestimated or underprepared for, because this is where vast amounts of value can be created. While there are several moving parts to an acquisition strategy, the benefits can be enormous, including:

Achieving market leadership and financial scale. This has significant benefits in various forms, including brand recognition, operating expense efficiencies, and a reduction in competitive forces.

Valuation multiple arbitrage. As a result of achieving scale, companies can generate valuation multiples as earnings are typically higher with lower volatility and greater predictability.

Increased exit opportunities. As scale increases, the number of buyers and the size of the buyers (both strategic and financial) also increase. Larger buyers often have higher valuations themselves and are able to pay more for companies they acquire.

LBO: case study—ABC Company to acquire XYZ Company

This case study walks through a sample LBO deal and provides an example of the qualitative and quantitative aspects of the LBO process that senior lenders should consider during the due diligence process. This process primarily takes a look at the role of the senior lender in regard to a deal structure for the revolver and the senior-secured term loan.

ABC Company has entered into an exclusive letter of intent (LOI) for the acquisition of all of the outstanding capital stock of XYZ Company from the shareholders of XYZ Company. Under the terms of the LOI, ABC Company has offered to acquire XYZ Company for $50 million. Based on the LOI, ABC Company is currently meeting with prospective lenders to support the consummation of the purchase. The following chart is a forecast of sources and uses for the transaction.

Sources:	Term	LIBOR+	Commit $	Closing $	TTM 2021A	7/31/22	2022F	Uses:	$
Revolver	5	3.75%	$ 2,000.00	$ –	0.00x	0.00x	0.00x	Pur. Price	$ 50,000
Senior – Term	5	3.75%		$ 24,000	3.61x	2.93x	2.74x	Trans costs	$ 1,500
Total Debt				$ 24,000					
Preferred Stock	n/a	0.00%		$ 23,500	7.14x	5.80x	5.41x		
Common Stock				$ 4,000	7.74x	6.29x	5.87x		
Total Equity				$ 27,500					
Total Sources				$ 51,500	7.74x	6.29x	5.87x	Total Uses	$ 51,500
Pre-Acquisition Enterprise Value / EBIDTA					7.51x	6.10x	5.70x		
Adjusted EBITDA					$6,665	$8,193	$8,775		

Company summary

XYZ Company offers outsourced accounts receivable collections, payment processing, and call center services to governmental entities and financial and higher education institutions nationwide. It provides a full suite of ARM solutions and empowers hundreds of employees with advanced technology, data management tools, and leading-edge business practices to increase the collections efficiency of its hundreds of nationwide government clients by raising collection rates and lowering costs. XYZ Company is a third-party collections agency and does not take ownership of any receivables and collects a contingent success fee (either fixed or percentage as an add-on or as a portion of the collection) based on the size and/or volume of transactions. The company is currently on track to generate revenue and adjusted EBITDA of $34.6 million (up 15.3 percent from $30 million from the previous year) and $8.8 million (up 31.9 percent from $6.7 million from the previous year), respectively.

XYZ Company's markets principally cover collections for government agencies, quasi-governmental agencies, and government-sponsored enterprises, and includes universities, toll roads, federal/state/county/city agencies requiring services such as court collections, debt collections, payment processing services, violation and citation enforcement, and photo enforcement (red light and toll, etc.), among others.

In the United States, there are approximately 7,000 accounts receivable collections firms, although less than 50 serve the government arena and less than 25 truly have the sophistication and infrastructure to meet the confidentiality, redundancy, and privacy required by government agencies.

Capital structure

Under the terms of the LOI, ABC Company has offered to acquire XYZ Company for $50 million. ABC Company is seeking a standby revolver of $2 million that will be undrawn at closing and will not likely be drawn in the normal course of operations (we anticipate XYZ Company will have $3 million of operating cash on the balance sheet at close), and a five-year senior term loan of $24 million. The $27.5 million of equity required to consummate the acquisition will be funded by ABC Company and its related entities. The structure of the equity investment has not been finalized, but it is anticipated that existing management will purchase ownership in the business for up to 20 percent. Furthermore, the founder of XYZ Company and a current board member intend to make a significant rollover equity investment alongside the investors in the company.

Based on the structure described previously, we believe we are seeking a conservative capital structure to support the growth and ongoing development of the business. A summary of the debt service coverage multiples is below.

FYI 12/31	F Opening	P 2022	P 2023	P 2024	P 2025	P 2026
Senior Debt	$24,000	$22,000	$17,200	$12,400	$7,600	$2,800
Senior Debt/ EBITDA	2.93x	2.51x	1.69x	1.08x	0.61x	0.21x
Total Debt/EBITDA	2.93x	2.51x	1.69x	1.08x	0.61x	0.21x
EBITDA/Total Interest		20.21x	10.07x	12.63x	17.46x	31.21x
Senior Debt/ (EBITDA-Capex)		2.74x	1.86x	1.17xx	0.66x	0.23x
Total Debt/ (EBITDA-Capex)		2.74x	1.86x	1.17x	0.66x	0.23x
Fixed Charger Coverage		3.15x	1.21x	1.37x	1.52x	1.67x

It should be noted that the tax structure of the transaction is undetermined. For the purposes of forecasting, we have used a 35 percent tax rate. This tax rate is reflected in the income statement and the fixed charge coverage calculations above.

Senior lender's viewpoint

The senior lender that is providing the revolver and senior term loan has considered several factors that have to do with macro deal issues and micro financial issues.

The macro issues tend to revolve around the five Cs of credit (character, capacity, capital, collateral, conditions). The senior lender asks the basic questions of whether the company's strategy and the franchise operators are prepared for the change ahead. The micro financial issues will consist of general lending requirements such as the financial pro-forma, capital, and the cash flow of the organization to ensure loan repayment is possible. In addition to the senior credit, the lender will want to ensure that the company will be able to sufficiently meet all debt obligations so the business will be operating on positive terms. Measuring debt ratios is key.

Reviewing proposed financials is critical, as well as understanding the coverage ratio. The coverage ratios determine the amount of EBITDA to interest and debt coverage and are critical relative to debt. Essentially, as long as the business is able to maintain an acceptable EBITDA, the business appears to have ample earnings to cover the debt service under most normal conditions.

In order to assess the total risk of the transaction, the senior lender on the revolver and senior term loan would also want to consider what level of decline in EBITDA would need to occur before the company's ability to repay principal and/or interest would be affected.

Going through the terms and conditions, they would most likely be in line with traditional LBO deals with one major exception: Since the organization is a franchise-based organization, the loan is primarily secured by cash flow versus assets. Thus, the bank could institute the ability to secure its position via the net fee to the franchisee. Since the revenue of the organization reports to the corporate office, the bank could reserve the right to increase the franchise fee by up to 5 percent until all principal and interest is repaid. This term alone would provide significant downside protection.

Lastly, the bank would want to understand its profitability on the loans. Based on this case study, this appears to be an attractive opportunity for the senior lender from a risk-return perspective and would most likely (subject to proper due diligence) represent a solid asset-deployment strategy for a banking organization that has asset-deployment strategy for the lender. The added term and condition of the increased franchise fee would give security on the bank's senior position, giving it the ability to recoup the loan proceeds with greater ease.

THE FUTURE OF LBOS

Over the past 30 years, the LBO experience has been a dynamic one. Banks, mezzanine providers, and private equity sponsors have profited from these transactions.

As the current markets continue to put pressure on organizations, the desire for larger companies to divest business units may become greater, and the aging of America will also create the need for more private company liquidity. These drivers will increase the LBO activity and may continue to take the use of LBOs to new heights.

As lenders review this marketplace, they consider the components in this book to determine if this is a market in which they want to participate. Their ability to understand the history, capital providers, capital structuring, and deal merits is critical to making the decision in providing LBO financing.

Overall, providing senior credit facilities to LBOs can be an attractive business for banks to enter into as it allows them a unique opportunity to deploy vast amounts of assets per deal and lowers the per deal cost friction associated with due diligence. For instance, it takes almost as much time and effort to underwrite a $25 million loan as it does a $100 million loan.

For private equity professionals the attraction to these transactions and the potential for significant carried interest rewards is likely to further compel acquisition activity. LBOs may take different shapes in the future, but this mega trend is likely to continue to play a major role in middle market transactions.

Chapter 4

THE RATIONALE FOR A DEAL

There are many reasons why a company seeks to grow through a merger or acquisition. Generally, a merger or acquisition is pursued for one of these two very broad strategies:

Growth in the same industry. The target business adds to an existing strength of the company, which means the buyer simply achieves more scale. When one auto company buys or merges with another auto company, it creates a bigger, stronger auto company. The experts who build cars would then be building more cars.

But just because the business lines are similar does *not* guarantee success. The 1990s "merger" (it was really a buyout) between

Daimler-Benz and Chrysler was a disaster, and both parties were miserable. But once the divorce was finalized, Chrysler soon found another partner in Fiat. The adoption of Chrysler by Fiat took place in 2014, and by all accounts the family is a happy one.

Entrance into a new industry. The target company adds something new, allowing the buyer to engage in activities or markets previously unavailable to them. When an auto company buys a financial services company, it creates an auto company that can operate a new line of business, issue its own credit cards, and make loans. The people who are experts at building cars are *not* experts at personal financial products, and therefore the finance company must operate with a certain degree of autonomy.

In an extreme form, this is what Warren Buffett does. Berkshire Hathaway is a big conglomerate, but it is operated as a holding company. It owns dozens of companies in industries including real estate, clothing, business services, fast food, insurance, motorcycles, media, toys—the list is dizzying. Buffett and his team take no part in the day-to-day operations of the businesses on the company's roster.

Within this general framework, here are the leading reasons for a business to seek a merger or acquisition.

Business model

The target's business model may be different from that of the buyer and so generates more profits. For example, a target may operate without labor unions or have a substantially less burdensome benefits plan. The buyer may not be able to recreate this business model in-house without suffering significant unrest but can readily buy into it through an acquisition.

Cyclicality reduction

A buyer may be trapped in a cyclical or seasonal industry where profitability fluctuates on a reoccurring basis. It may deliberately acquire a company outside this industry with the goal of offsetting the business cycle to yield more consistent financial results. For example, a company that manufactures lawn mowers might be interested in buying a company that makes snowblowers.

In a more cynical take on this concept, in 2009, Reynolds American, the second-largest tobacco company in the United States and the maker of Camel cigarettes, paid $44 million to buy a Swedish company, Niconovum, that made nicotine gum and other nicotine replacement products designed to help smokers quit. This meant that Reynolds would sell smokers their cigarettes . . . and when the consumer wanted to quit smoking, Reynolds would sell them the nicotine replacement they needed.

Defensive

Some acquisitions take place because the buyer is itself the target of another company and simply wants to make itself less attractive through an acquisition. This is particularly effective when the buyer already has a large market share and buying another entity in the same market gives it such a large share that it cannot be bought by anyone else in the industry without antitrust charges being brought.

Executive compensation

A buyer's management team may be in favor of an acquisition for the simple reason that a larger company generally pays higher salaries. The greater heft of the resulting organization is frequently viewed as valid grounds for a significant pay boost among the surviving management team. This is not a good reason for an acquisition, but it is a common one.

Intellectual property

This is a defensible knowledge base that gives a company a competitive advantage and is one of the best reasons to acquire a company. Intellectual property can include patents, trademarks, production processes, and databases that are difficult to recreate, and research and development labs with a history of successful product development.

For example, in 2012, Apple purchased Authentec, a company that provided security hardware and software for PCs and mobile devices. Authentec boasted an extensive range of patents, with over 200 filed and issued in the United States. Its patent portfolio ranged from biometric fingerprint sensor technology to embedded security devices. As part of the buyout, Apple agreed to pay a $7.5 million fee for "engineering services," and any new intellectual property coming out of Authentec would be the sole property of Apple.

Internal development alternative

A company may have an extremely difficult time creating new products. This issue is especially likely to trigger an acquisition if a company has just decided to cancel an in-house development project and needs a replacement immediately.

Local market expertise

In some industries, effective entry into a local market requires the gradual accumulation of reputation through a long process of building contacts and correct business practices. A company can follow this path through internal expansion and gain success over a long period of time—or do it at once through an acquisition. Local market expertise is especially valuable in international situations, when a buyer has minimal knowledge of local customs, not to mention the inevitable obstacles posed by a different language.

Market growth

No matter how hard a buyer may push itself, it simply cannot grow revenues very fast in a slow-growth market because there are so few sales to be made. Conversely, a target company may be situated in a market that is growing much faster than that of the buyer, so the buyer sees an avenue to more rapid growth.

Market share

Companies strive toward a high market share because this generally allows them to enjoy a cost advantage over their competitors, who must spread their overhead costs over smaller production volumes. The acquisition of a large competitor is a reasonable way to quickly attain significant market share.

Production capacity

Though not a common acquisition justification, the buyer may have excess production capacity available from which it can readily manufacture the target's products. Usually, machinery, equipment, and process differences between companies make this a difficult, but possible endeavor.

Products

The target may have an excellent product the buyer can use to fill a hole in its own product line. This is an especially important reason when the market is expanding rapidly, and the buyer does not have sufficient time to develop the product internally before other competing products take over the market.

Regulatory environment

The buyer may be burdened by a suffocating regulatory environment, such as those imposed on utilities, airlines, and government contractors.

Sales channels

A target may have an unusually effective sales channel that the buyer thinks it can use to distribute its own products. Examples of such sales channels are as varied as door-to-door sales, electronic downloads, telemarketing, or a well-trained in-house sales staff. Also, the target's sales staff might be especially effective. In some industries, the sales department is considered the bottleneck operation and may be the prime reason for an acquisition offer.

Vertical integration

A company may want to strengthen its supply chain by acquiring selected suppliers. This is especially important if there is considerable demand for key supplies and a supplier has control over a large proportion of them, and it is of even more consequence when suppliers are located in politically volatile areas, leaving few reliable suppliers. In addition to this "backward integration," a company can also engage in "forward integration" by acquiring a distributor or customer. This most commonly occurs with distributors, especially if they have unusually excellent relationships with the ultimate set of customers.

WHAT MAKES A TARGET WANT TO SELL

Just as there are many reasons why a company would look to acquire another, there are many reasons why a company might want to offer itself for sale.

Anemic profits

If a target has minimal or no profits, it cannot sustain itself. In this scenario, a buyer may complete an acquisition for a low price and then have to restructure the acquisition in order to dredge up a profit.

Competitive environment

The number and aggressiveness of a target's competitors may have increased substantially, resulting in a current or impending revenue and profit decline. While a buyer can often obtain such a company for a reduced price, they must also question whether they want to enter into such a difficult environment.

Estate taxes

The owner of a company may have died, and his estate must sell the business in order to pay estate taxes. The deceased owner's relatives may not have a clear idea of the value of the company so a prospective buyer may have a relatively easy time negotiating with an inexperienced counterpart.

Patent expiration

A company may be selling products and/or services in a protected environment, using a key patent that keeps competitors at bay. However, that patent is now close to expiration, and the target is not sure if it will be able to compete effectively.

Rapid growth

A company may be growing so fast that it cannot obtain sufficient working capital to support the growth of the business. This scenario is a good one. Since the company has proof of strong growth, it may be able to negotiate a higher price.

Retirement

A company owner wants to retire and needs to cash out in order to do so. If the owner has established a long timeline for the sale, he can sort through a variety of offers and negotiate at length, resulting in a higher price. Conversely, a rushed retirement timeline can often force down the price.

Shareholder pressure

If a company is privately held, then its shareholders will have a difficult time selling their stock. A buyer can provide complete liquidity to these shareholders either through an all-cash offer or by issuing shares that can be registered for sale to other investors. This is an especially common reason when the management team does not hold majority ownership of the target's shares and therefore cannot control the decision.

Stalled growth

A company may find that its growth has been stalled for any number of reasons. Maximized revenue is a logical point at which to sell, so the target puts itself up for sale on the assumption that a buyer can reinvigorate growth.

Technological obsolescence

A company may have based its core business on a technology that is now becoming obsolete, and it cannot afford the overhaul required for advancement or replacement.

This is a big piece of the classic story of Blockbuster. In the early 1990s, under the leadership of Wayne Huizenga, Blockbuster became a multibillion-dollar video rental company. But Huizenga foresaw how new technology, including video on demand (VOD) and the growth of cable television, could threaten the business. In 1991, just three days after Time Warner announced it would upgrade its cable system, Blockbuster's shares dropped more than 10 percent. In 1994, unable to come up with a solution to counteract the growing threats to the traditional video store, he made the decision to sell Blockbuster to Viacom for $8.4 billion. Smart move—while Blockbuster continued to grow and reached its peak in 2004, its business model was obsolete. On September 23, 2010, Blockbuster filed for Chapter 11 bankruptcy protection due to challenging losses, $900 million in debt, and strong competition from Netflix, Redbox, and VOD services.

STRATEGIC PLANNING

Strategic planning is important throughout all aspects of a company's life cycle. As market conditions change and new technologies emerge, it is important for businesses to plan for these changes and react accordingly, making adjustments and pivots along the way.

Almost any company can find itself in an unfortunate situation. One of the examples we often refer to is Eastman Kodak and Fujifilm. One ended up in bankruptcy after decades of industry leadership, while the other came from behind to become an industry dominator. This difference in outcome stemmed merely from subtle changes over time. This is why a well-thought-through strategy is so important, as it will help the company navigate the competitive environment effectively.

The use of capital itself is not the strategy. The strategy is the strategy. While that sounds overly simplistic, it is important to keep in mind that actions including raising capital, mergers, and acquisitions should be done to *fulfill* the organization's strategy.

Chapter 5

PREPARING FOR
THE SALE OF A COMPANY

The decision to sell a company is never an easy process, both emotionally as well as from a working perspective. However, once that decision has been made, there are things that should take place to better prepare the company for an exit. Whether the sale is going to happen in the same calendar year or two or three years down the road, the more time there is to prepare for the sale of the business or for taking on growth capital, the better.

Prepare financials

Although a broad topic, finance includes customer billing, capital management, bank account management, cash flow management, and more. This information should be available, accurate, and easy to work with. On the buyer's end, they will verify the financials provided via a third party such as an audit firm.

Business intelligence

A company should understand each component of its financial statement, which items can be tracked, which items are going out of the business, how the business can be affected, and what levers can be pulled in the company to create profitability. Business intelligence may be, for example, a customer relationship management (CRM) system that accurately portrays pricing, or a future projection model that shows backlog and booked jobs relative to booked revenue, which would help with understanding different pricing metrics with vendors.

Regardless of which type is chosen, each component of the financial statements should have some level of business intelligence to it, so that by product or service, the company can drill down and understand the key moving factors for the business.

Creating defensibility

Whether it is intellectual property, trademarks, copyrights, or exclusives, having contracts in place with vendors and customers in defense of a company's product is key so somebody cannot easily come along and sideswipe their product or service.

Marketplace analysis

This is a good thing to be doing on a regular basis, regardless of preparing for a sale or not. It should be a general business item and done a couple of times per year. It is important to have a finger on all the things that move and change the customer dynamic and their purchasing attitudes. These include pricing competition, areas of improvement, trends, etc. A company should be able to easily explain the levers that move the needle in their marketplace to anybody wanting to invest in or buy out their firm.

Management team preparations

It is important to have the right management team in place and also to make sure that the team is prepared for a sale transaction. This can be done by ensuring the management team is fully set up, their contracts are in place, and interests are aligned prior to, during, and after the transaction.

Legal

This includes important items such as good corporate standing, liens, contracts, leases, and so on. All of these things should be buttoned up and correctly executed, as they will all be reviewed and inspected in very granular detail. Several of those will come out during the audit process, so it is important to be prepared.

Capitalization table

This should be organized from the start and be well tracked and well taken care of. It should also be all-encompassing, meaning that employee grants, options, verbal commitments, and written commitments are all taken into account. Investor classes and amounts per class should be well documented and well structured in the capital table. A waterfall calculation should be kept up-to-date based on the approximate enterprise value of the company. Lastly, the different components of the capitalization table should be labeled to tie back to the documents and legal agreements for which they have been accounted.

PREPARING FOR CAPITAL DEALS

Each CEO has many tasks and responsibilities; however, making sure that a capital deal can be made is one of the greatest.

Every company should be ready for capital, whether they need it now or later. Preparing the company for a capital event, whether it is a sale and infusion of bank loan proceeds or an investment for private equity, is imperative for all stakeholders (including employees and customers). Secondly, every business has cycles. Understanding when to take advantage of the cycle and deploy capital for growth, when to pull back, and when to exit are essential parts of the job for every CEO. It is important to take a look into sales that provide ultimate computational value of the company and into capital investments that make a current statement about the company condition or value.

Similarly, understanding the difference between opportunities and needs can help you make the right decision when it comes to raising capital. Though you might have an opportunity available for a capital raise, it is imperative to have a purpose behind it, for many reasons.

For one, it is extremely important to be able to communicate your purpose with clarity to those from whom you are asking for capital.

Secondly, it is important to understand the types of markets and parties you will need to have for your deal.

Finally, it is important to have a strong plan in action because going through the process of obtaining capital is never easy, whether it is a bank loan or the ultimate exit of a company. It will test the patience of every company owner, and without a driving purpose, some business owners will get frustrated and give up shy of reaching their goal of obtaining capital, even though the goal was actually obtainable.

Steps in the process of a capital deal

Now, let's take a look at how to begin the process. There are three key features to begin a capital process and complete a deal in the capital markets.

1. Take a calculated risk.

Anytime you enter into a capital process, there is usually some form of associated risk, and making sure that this risk is calculated is key as CEO.

2. Prepare the required documents.

Make sure that the materials, financials, due diligence, and company information are prepared as best as possible in order to build confidence in your message and requests.

3. Understand the desired outcome.

Because of the difficulty it takes to arrange bank debt all the way to an exit, it is important to have a good understanding of what outcome is truly important to you. Merely testing the waters is usually a waste of time, and it is better to have a vision when shaping your philosophy.

The following are some of the key questions to address:

- With whom do you want to be in business and why?
- What are you really trying to accomplish with bringing in capital?
- What does life in business look like after you have closed the deal?
- Post-closing, what has to happen in the next three to five years to have made the capital to make the deal a long-term success?
- Are you ready to lead the company and start a process in that direction today? If not, then why, when, and what is really holding you back?

Understanding your own philosophy of entering into a deal is as important as any other feature. Having that crystal-clear purpose as

CEO will help direct the company forward to the capital partners and ultimately close a deal.

Time killers

When preparing for capital, there are several time killers that can be a drain on your emotions, intellect, and schedule.

Doing too much DIY

Attempting to coordinate a deal by yourself is not the way to approach it. It is important to understand all the legal, accounting, investment, and banking contacts in order to help you secure the right form of capital for your company and legal structure.

Thinking too small

Many times, we see companies that think too small and look for forms of capital that are not going to meet their long-term needs. In some cases, these can be more difficult to get than larger amounts of capital that would better meet their needs.

Having unrealistic expectations

Professionalism is born from having both realistic and obtainable capital goals relative to the size of the company, cycle of the company, the need for capital, and the means to create a return back on that capital. This is where having an investment banker or valuation expert can provide you with thoughts on what is appropriate for the type of business you run relative to leverage amounts and capital requirements.

Fishing in a dry pond

Many times, we see clients that have tried to run a process on their own and have been talking with capital providers, whether banks or private equity groups or individual investors, that are never going to issue them capital. It is important to speak with the right people at the right time.

Being too timid

It is good to be humble, but sometimes being too timid in a capital request can come across as unsure or unprepared. That is why going through the process of preparing documents and having a clear purpose is so important for a CEO. When you are talking with various parties that might have an interest in investing in your company, you must try to attain the perfect balance of being confident yet humble at the same time.

Negotiating on the wrong points

Many times, early deals are beginning to take root, but a CEO starts negotiating on different points of a deal too early and focuses on the wrong points. This tends to have a large backfire effect as it can cause the capital provider to push back from the table and not be engaged. It is important to understand when it is time to negotiate certain points and when it is time to leave certain items alone.

KEY COMMUNICATION ELEMENTS OF A DEAL

Marketing and communication are two key factors in achieving a successful capital raise or deal. Effective marketing and communication invoke a learning process in consumers and build overall confidence in your brand. Through time and methodological communication, interested potential capital providers or buyers should develop more of a comprehensive understanding of your company.

This is what we refer to as the *funnel*. On the top of the funnel, you paint a picture of the macro landscape of your vertical. You should be aware of how and why your company is going to grow or why its environment is shrinking. For example, if you say your business is growing, but it is in a shrinking vertical, people want to know why your company is going to be growing outside the growth vertical. You then narrow down the details and ultimately narrow down and complete a deal.

Below are several key communication pieces that are used as part of this funnel.

Teaser/executive summary

This is a blind viewing of the company to be shared with prospective parties/investors/buyers, typically presented as a one- or two-page overview or summary of the business. A teaser typically starts by highlighting the industry at a macro level and includes specific advantages the company has as well as a high-level financial overview. Again, this is meant to be blind, so including graphs is one way to effectively show some of this information without including specific numbers and details. It is okay if it is a little less descriptive, as it only is meant to engage the reader and draw them into the second portion of the process, which is reviewing an NDA to potentially sign.

Nondisclosure agreement (NDA)

The NDA has language that allows the potential capital partner to sign it as is. It should be complex enough to convey sincerity and mutual enough to communicate fairness and transparency. If the NDA is not conveyed well, it can be taken as an initial signal that you are going to be difficult to deal with as time goes on. If the NDA is too simplistic, it communicates that you are not taking the process very seriously, and in that case, why should the other party?

Confidential information memorandum (CIM)

The confidential information memorandum (CIM) is a comprehensive document that includes a wide range of information about the company, management, team, resources, operations, financials, industry, market landscape, growth plan and forecast, and more. It is important that the CIM is of the utmost visual and informational quality as possible. For the financial section of the CIM, it is best to have three years of historical data and five years of projections. Be consistent, be defensible, and be accurate.

Data room

The data room is typically an online hub of information about the company and should include any and all items necessary to complete a due diligence review. The data room should include, but not be limited to, legal documentation, including the articles of incorporation, partnership agreements, financial detail, and backup of the company's financials in much more detail than initially provided in the CIM. Audit information and review feedback and data can serve as strong testaments to your company as can significant customers, any major contracts, organization charts, insurance plans, and human resource-related items for benefit plans, each of which can be included in the data room to assist in the due diligence process.

Management meeting

This meeting includes potential investors and other interested parties, and it is one of the most misunderstood components of the deal process. We regularly see people that either put too much emphasis or formality on it or not enough.

It is important that the management meeting conveys several things:

- **Courtesy and charisma**. People want to do business with people they like.

- **Competence of management**. Management should be prepared to share insights into the company and industry. This is especially important if management will be staying involved in the company. And, if that is the case, management should use the management meeting as an opportunity to convey a sense of vision for the company's future and growth as well as the ability to lead. Both of these can be very attractive to investors.

- **Confidence**. Demonstrate "thoughtful confidence" in the company. Be careful not to be arrogant, however, as that is always a major red flag to investors.

Preparation

When preparing for a management meeting, there are a few things that every management team can do to increase the odds of having a successful meeting and presentation. Some of these things are inherent in the general pitches that companies might do for enterprise customers or larger customers, but for companies that do not typically go through these pitches, management meetings can be quite intimidating.

Create a clear, visually powerful presentation version of the CIM and include additional information as needed.

Practice. Practice. Practice. Even if you're a skilled presenter, you should practice what you plan to say in advance of the meeting.

When you practice your pitch, focus on giving a solid delivery by reducing the amount of "ums" and "uhs." Know when to inflect your voice, when to pause, when to get excited, and when to be mundane. Practice slide by slide until you can effectively deliver each one.

Once you have mastered what you're going to say, your last preparation task is to connect all the dots throughout the whole presentation. Each slide should not be a completely new story but should connect to the overall story. Making each slide its own reference point is a big mistake. Your presentation should have fluidity from slide to slide, section to section, and presenter to presenter, and it should ultimately build upon itself.

Everyone in the management meeting should be on the same page with what is being presented. Be sure to review all the materials and have a few prepared statements on finance, operations, and growth for high-level discussions.

Presentation format

In terms of format, your presentation should have two or three important ideas on each slide that support your overarching pitch. Things such as growth, market position dominance, increasing margins, stickiness of customers, stickiness of revenue, and so on really start to build confidence in investors, especially if they are paired with hooks. The hooks do not have to be overt, but they need to suggest that the company has an attractive position. Each slide is going to have some type of reference as to why the company is unique, special, and attractive, so it is important to go through each slide and customize each hook.

Following are the agenda items, in order, for a typical meeting.

TYPICAL MEETING AGENDA
DURING A CAPITAL DEAL

1. **Introductions.** It is customary to have a brief but well-highlighted intro (name, title, description of role/responsibilities, relevant background/education). The introductions should also set up for responses to Q&A so that when you get to Q&A, there is a natural lead person to respond to certain questions. It is important to keep introductions to two minutes or less per person and to provide enough information to make a connection and establish credibility.

2. **Site walk.**

3. **Company overview "story."**

4. **General Q&A/Capital provider key questions addressed.** Based on the intros and roles, you should let the party best suited respond to each question, and then others can chime in to add color. Clear, succinct answers build confidence in the investor group as they are more

continued

likely to actually understand what is being discussed. It is ideal to limit responses to one to two minutes and avoid 10-minute answers, which can often create more questions than answers. If you are stumped by a question or it might require more time or information to answer, it's okay to respond, "Let me get the information together, and I will communicate back to you in greater depth." Doing this is better than struggling around a topic or not having an answer.

5. **Wrap-up.** It is important to reserve a few minutes for a casual wrap-up for people to shake hands and connect individually if possible. On the phone, a gracious goodbye and "Look forward to meeting you in person" or a little humor is always a plus.

Management meeting reminders

Think of the management meeting as:

- A key relationship-building opportunity. The most important part of the meeting is to develop a positive relationship, as you might be partnered with your capital provider for many years and will likely share business ups and downs, meetings, and decision making together. Therefore, it is important for the meeting to have an overall positive tone.

- A mutual interview. The management meeting is a component of your capital partner's due diligence. They will be assessing the management team, business, growth opportunities, and the overall working relationship of your firm, and you will be doing some of the same. Be on point with your information and responses, and although you are also interviewing them, make it your aim to build conviction that your firm is a solid investment.

Deal-selling statements

Deal-selling statements are "dot connectors." They are meant to encourage alignment of interests and a vision of what the company is doing today combined with future plans and direction. Deal-selling statements are important to plan and practice in advance. Examples of common types of deal-selling statements are:

- "The growth of the business is clear, realistic, and concise" (use stats and figures to back up statements).

- "Macroeconomics are in favor of the industry for the foreseeable future."

- "There are repetitive known clients, cash flows, and overall financial predictability" (within reason).

- "We have a depth of market understanding and landscape."

- "We have a cohesive management team that is focused on growing the business."

Deal-killing statements

Deal-killing statements are those that are disjointed from materials already presented, disjointed from what you are doing now, and disjointed from the future you want to create. They often present a problem or an issue but fail to provide an immediate solution.

There are probably more deal-killing statements made in meetings than deal-making statements, but it's important that consistency and communication exist, as that leads to a more credible message. Examples of common types of deal-killing statements are:

- Bringing up unknown risk that has not been discussed and there is no plan to cure
- Macros moving against the industry
- Unclear growth path
- Information that contradicts prior information in a negative way
- Management team dysfunction

Other important items

Dress. Simply wearing a "nice version" of what you would normally wear to the office is fine. It is not necessary to overdress for these meetings.

Facility and office. It is worth spending the time to organize and clean a little more than normal before the meeting. How you keep your company facility says something about how you run your company. Also, capital providers always like to see a company in action, so having work going on is a plus.

Meals. If there will be a dinner or lunch off-site, it is important to make reservations so the meal process goes smoothly. If the meal will be catered, the food should be scheduled in advance so it arrives on time.

Distractions and interruptions. The initial management meeting is a vital underwriting step for any investor. It is important that this meeting has your team's undivided attention and that staff are aware of this. Generally, there will be one or two scheduled breaks for a quick email check or returned phone call.

It is hard to skip any step in this communication process and still have a successful deal, as each of these steps has been set up to continually build on one another and communicate understanding and confidence.

Fast-tracking a deal too much can hurt the process, so be sure to go through each step and focus on executing them well.

SPECIAL CASES: DISTRESSED COMPANIES

We will end this chapter with a special section on distressed companies. Fortunately—or unfortunately—I have had the opportunity to work with several distressed companies on restructuring, equity placements, and mergers and acquisitions, and there are a few hard-and-fast rules I have seen play out time and time again with each scenario.

In a distressed scenario, the company is often over-leveraged, undercapitalized, and has suffered from lost revenue. When all of that occurs, a combination of things go through a CEO's head. There is often some holding on to the past and some looking forward to a brighter future, but often there is a disconnect between the past, future, and present.

Many times, this scenario is a result of having many assets and expenses relative to what the company requires. The owner may have a hard time letting go of certain assets and certain personnel because they believed that these assets and people would be necessary in the future. That form of thinking can be detrimental to a company's financial health.

Here is a quick playbook for a distressed scenario, either in your company or a subsidiary you are buying.

Shed unneeded assets

First and foremost, shed unneeded assets. Sell the unneeded assets if there is an available market for them, but do not chase your tail trying to sell things you cannot sell. It is important to do this step right out of the gate because as time goes on, the distress often gets worse. It typically drives down the value of those assets while the speed and need of liquidity increases. These things are inversely correlated—as your need for the liquidity increases, the liquidity price decreases.

Reduce staff

With asset sales, you may be able to justify keeping staff slightly longer to help with those sales, but the next step is to look at a possible reduction in staffing. This is one of the most painful things a business leader can do, but it is absolutely necessary for the financial health of a company once it has had a revenue upset. Accurately sizing a business to its realistic financial and revenue reality is important.

Focus on regrowth

Through good pricing and good customer relationships, you can begin focusing on the regrowth of the company. When it comes to pricing, one temptation is thinking that any revenue is good revenue. To some degree that can be true in certain companies such as higher-margin businesses, but in other companies that philosophy and way of thinking can be the ultimate thing that kills the company.

For instance, for a software company with high margins, every dollar is a good dollar, but for a manufacturing business, there will be wear and tear on machines, and the pricing needs to cover mainte-nance costs or new investments in the future. If the pricing fails to do so, there will be no profit left, and all it is really doing is covering a bit of overhead, which is a scenario conducive for a complete financial meltdown. Additionally, discounting can often hurt in the long run as it affects the company's brand and overall perception of the com-pany and its offerings (products/services).

Choose the right partners

During this time period, working with lenders and equity pro-viders can be very stressful. Some lenders will be willing to work with certain companies, and other lenders will not. Sometimes it is appropriate to look at switching from a bank to a credit fund that is used to dealing with distressed situations. Managing that first lien relationship is absolutely critical because at any given point in time, lenders can make a distressed scenario either a lot worse or a lot easier to deal with.

Maintaining open dialogue and candid conversations with equity providers is also important. Many times, if the relationship is good and the management team has been forthright with the equity pro-vider, additional capital can be invested. Other resources that can be deployed include buying another company or merging into another portfolio company, both of which could have benefits to the business and preserve shareholder value.

Liquidations are also unfortunate happenings that, with a certain level of distress, might be a reality.

Next steps

After stabilizing the company, what are some of the pathways to completely get out of distress? One is simply to go into what we would call a proactively dormant state, in which the company is stabilized and has created enough cash and operating cash flow to get through a year or two of delivering the business.

Typically, this is a company that does a great job of servicing customers but to some degree, in terms of new investments and so forth, remains financially dormant as it looks to slowly rebuild. This is a path that many companies take during this stage and emerge successful. Be patient during this stage as it might take a three- to five-year vision to return the company to where it once was.

Another path could be to find a positive equity partner and look for ways to acquire other companies individually or through a roll-up. Personally, I would look for a company that could provide helpful infrastructure. Acquiring a company of a large size—or one that was previously of large size—can usually recreate some of the resources and budgets that were once available.

Lastly, a distressed company could consider merging with or selling to another company, either for cash or equity. Sometimes prior strategies that the company utilized getting the company back on its original path can be so long and difficult that management teams' and shareholders' time frames are mismatched. This is when it is best for the company to be sold or merged into another company, where there can be product or service synergies, rather than risk experiencing time delays and stressors both emotionally and financially.

Chapter 6

GETTING TO THE CLOSE

There are many aspects to the close, and this chapter details the most crucial ones.

DUE DILIGENCE

When it comes to due diligence, there is a fairly standard playbook for most lenders, private credit, and private equity funds. Each diligence item will be thoroughly reviewed and methodically dissected to better understand the mechanics for how the company conducts itself relative to its financials. I provide a detailed checklist of due diligence items in Appendix C at the end of this book.

Third-party diligence usually centers around quality of earnings, which is a review and tracking of the financial statement relative to what has been shared with the capital providers. Essentially, they are looking to verify the information that has been shared. It is like a mini audit, if you will. They review revenue, customer accounts, invoices, and so forth. All tie back to the bank account and actual deposits.

Additionally, it is common in the diligence process to go through non-balance sheet audits such as employee benefit programs, insurance, and legal, all of which depend on intellectual property, the type of business, and the complexities of the business involved. For instance, the more robust the benefits program, the more likely there would be an audit of the employee benefits program.

Similarly, the more extensive the intellectual property of the company, the more likely there is to be an extensive IP review.

So, whatever the major focuses or drivers are, you should expect a group to do more diligence in those areas to make sure they cover their bases. It's important with diligence not to overreact or get stressed out about it. Due diligence is merely a part of the deal process and can be largely mitigated if you run your company a certain way prior to the diligence, such as having regular bare minimum audits. Organizationally, it is important to make sure that i's are dotted and t's are crossed, but at the end of the day, due diligence is nothing to be intimidated by, as it is merely a process of gathering and checking information.

There are no deals out there where a capital provider or buyer investor gives money without doing sensitive due diligence. I would argue that if there is such a deal, this would be a sign of future problems to come. Little work on the front end can usually mean a lot of problems on the back end.

LEGAL

Legal can be an arduous process at times, but, like due diligence, it is a necessary part of the process. It is imperative that a company has not only good legal representation but a good deal of quality, experienced representation. Commonly, if everything goes well, there is very little looking back at legal documents and very little need for them.

Legal documents serve as a guidepost for how the relationship will exist going forward, for controls during the process, and for detailing what happens upon a liquidity event. Those three things are some of the most important aspects in a legal document. These benefits are amplified with quality representation.

The legal documents can oftentimes be quite confusing. Financial and structural terms and conditions can often be different than what is in a term sheet or initial indication; they may be tighter, looser, or just different. Spending time with the legal documents and making sure that all parties agree with their contents can help ease some of this confusion.

FINANCIAL PERFORMANCE

One of the important management strategies that a CEO must deploy when going through the process is asking the question, "How will we keep financial performance high going into the last two months before a close?" Once the capital partner has been selected and you are marching toward a close, nothing can change the deal faster than showing up with poor financial performance. It is important to stay within the modeling assumptions that have been provided to the capital partner in the deal.

A lot of these assumptions do have downside scenarios, which may be 10 percent, 15 percent, or more below where the model is operating. If the company is performing sluggishly and operating below the downside scenario, the delta in those scenarios can make a deal undoable, meaning that the downside performance in the downside scenario makes the company too risky. To prevent this outcome, it is important that modeling assumptions are realistic. There is no extra credit for trading financial models that are unrealistic, and if anything, it is a question of credibility and honesty. If your models are bolstered and not realistic, they can be a threat to the management team's integrity.

RE-TRADES

Whether you are raising capital or doing an M&A transaction, it is a fair assumption that some component of the deal will change as you go through the process. Deals do frequently close at a letter of intent or at the term sheet terms, but things can come up during the diligence process, as the capital provider learns more, and as their understanding deepens.

Re-trading is the practice of renegotiating the deal price of a company after the initial price and terms have been agreed to. This occurs when the buyer performs due diligence during negotiations and uncovers potential risks.

The capital provider can look at the structure of the deal and potentially re-trade certain components of it. There is a point of no return for a company looking to raise capital or to sell a business—a point that capital providers can easily recognize—and this is why maintaining financial performance is so critical.

It is best to go into any process under the impression that the closed deal will likely tilt toward the capital provider's way, away from the term sheet. That being said, effective preparation can reduce this tilt.

MENTALITY OF THE CLOSE

The reality of a close, unlike the movies out there or many celebrated stories in the financial press, is oftentimes fairly anticlimactic. The big thing we try to stress with clients is to focus on getting the close done. It is important to stay focused on getting it right at close, because starting over almost always will require more costs, more time, more delays, and more risk than moving forward with a transaction. Once committed, it is important to go into a close being open to some minor give-and-take in order to get to a place where all parties feel there is enough benefit to move forward. The compromises should be in the middle versus tilted to one side or the other.

Here are a few examples of situations when the "just get it closed" attitude would have been the right choice.

My organization and I were looking to sell an owner's company. Based on the comps and the different groups participating in the business, we had valued the company at $40 million. All of the offers we received came back in the mid-$30 million range. It was a good process with multiple offers and a tight pattern, but the owner decided to walk away from the table over what amounted to be a $4 million or $5 million difference in perceived value versus market feedback value. In the end, a combination of health issues and a downtick in business saw the owner lose about half of the company's EBITDA over the forward 12 months after the walkaway. This resulted in its new valuation being closer to $20 million.

For another example, let's go back to the Great Recession of 2008. During the financial crisis, I was working for an organization that presented a letter of intent to another company and wanted to quickly get started on diligence. The offer was for $14.5 million. We went back and forth, with the owner ultimately saying his company was worth $18.5 million. We appreciated his thoughts, but from our vantage point, that was not a realistic valuation. This was in early 2008, and within six months, the financial crisis had gone into full steam. By 2010, that company was only worth around $5 million.

Although this is a rather extreme example, it goes to show that it is sometimes not worth being too stringent with an amount or letting a small term get in the way of getting a deal done. With a "just get it closed" attitude, that particular company and its shareholder base could have had a significant payout at close opposed to what they ended up with.

We have seen the flip side to be true as well, when people held out and achieved better deals. It does happen, but as a colleague of mine likes to say, "Country clubs are filled with people who sold too early and took the 'get it closed' approach."

DEAL FATIGUE

As going through diligence information and legal documents goes on for weeks or months, it's not uncommon to feel an element of deal fatigue. To avoid it, it is important to prepare from the start.

Surround the CEO with a team

This team may be expensive, but relative to alternatives and ultimate value, a good team can create more value and be worth the costs. This team typically consists of the CFO, an investment banker, a tax/audit firm, a legal team, HR resources, and also may include outside consultants. The overall goal of the team is to handle much of the day-to-day of getting the deal to closing. This allows the CEO and management team to focus on continuing to run the company, which, as we have discussed, is imperative. Staying on track financially, staying within budget, keeping revenue, and growing expenses (within budget) are all important factors for going into a successful close, but to do so, a solid team needs to be in place.

Clear expectations

When it comes to a deal, it's important for everyone involved to have clear expectations and lean toward taking the conservative approach to those expectations. Be patient and conservative with timelines and understand that diligence may be a long process. Trying to rush the process can often end up making the overall process take longer.

Regularly scheduled communications

It can be helpful to set up 15 minutes a day in the morning or evening to go through updates as a team rather than have random ad hoc discussions throughout the day, which can be disjointing and disconnecting. Have systematic approaches to communication and execute with appropriate measures of intensity. There may be the occasional time when texting on a Sunday morning or Friday evening may be appropriate, but those moments should only really occur near the end of the process.

Maintaining a reasonable level of communication allows team members to have stamina and maintain healthy relationships throughout the entire process to a successful close. Communication intensity should have an upward slope as heavy upfront intensity will create deal fatigue quickly and lead to a poorly executed deal.

TRAITS OF FAILED DEALS

There are several traits that are consistent in failed deals. Along the road of deal destruction, they can be separated into two basic statements with several subcategories. The two main categories, which encapsulate roughly 95 percent of the reasons why deals fail, are: 1) the market does not appreciate the opportunity, or 2) the company does not appreciate the market. The other 5 percent can be attributed to events such as management transitions, death, divorce, or even simple changes of heart.

The market does not appreciate the opportunity

Let's dig into some of the subcategories of why the market may fail to appreciate the opportunity.

Poor presentation

Sometimes this can emerge from the way a company is presented. We have seen many business brokerage deals that were presented merely by a simple flyer, almost like selling a piece of real estate. This poor packaging and overall poor presentation of the company can make it unattractive and not seem worthy of institutional investors and buyers. If a company is buttoned up, has the right financial profile, and is in a solid vertical, it also needs to look the part in order to be taken seriously.

Lack of preparation

Preparation is key in being attractive to investors. Not having quick and easy access to financial information, missing components such as an HR handbook, or having outstanding tax issues or liens all can impair the company's ability to attract an investor and get an offer.

Making outlandish claims

Once you get into diligence, some materials may suggest outlandish claims for growth. This is generally a huge mistake because, for one thing, it sets an expectation that may be very unrealistic, but most importantly it brings into question the credibility of the information purveyor. If the company has been at $15 million per year of sales for the last three years and your information suggests that sales are going to go to $20 million in the following year without changing anything, that really brings into question the credibility of management. Why, after three years of stagnation, is there going to be a major change?

Manage and present your company and growth expectations with a pound of optimism, but also balance it with a sense of realism to make sure that there is credibility.

Underappreciated verticals

It is possible that the market may just underappreciate certain verticals or geographic locations. This can be a stumbling block but can be somewhat prepared for. For instance, if your company is three or four hours away from a local airport, that will not work for some institutional investors. A remedy could be to show an investor the path to move the company to a more desirable geographic location.

Scale

For many institutional investors and buyers, there are lines in the sand when it comes to financial size and revenue. For some, it is actually written in their documents that they cannot invest in a company below a certain amount of EBITDA. In the modern day, many funds and investors that have an institutional quality will start to be interested in a company that has over $2 million of EBITDA. This number may go down for an add-on or an investment, but typically it is around the $2 million EBITDA mark. The next rung goes up to roughly $5 to $10 million. This is really where the true lower middle market begins and where you start to see more interest from a full array of international, national, regional, and local investment/capital providers who have an institutional quality.

The company does not appreciate the market

There are various subcategories as to why the company may fail to appreciate the market.

Valuation

In my experience, there commonly can be a valuation issue that rests on the seller's shoulders, typically stemming from unrealistic expectations. Seeing that Uber got up to 8x revenue as their valuation, an owner might not understand why their local company that does $10 million in revenue might not be worth $80 million. It is important to stay informed on the deals and multiples that are happening in your respective industry; otherwise you might miss out on a great offer due to uninformed expectations.

Re-trade

As said before, it is common for certain elements initially determined in the beginning of a deal to be altered or thrown out. During diligence, certain items might arise that were unknown to the investor or buyer, which may add to or take away from the value of a company. This can happen especially when, during the process of the deal, the financial performance of the company starts significantly escalating or dropping off.

Naturally, a downward alteration in valuation may cause a seller to pull back from the deal, which, in my experience, is usually a mistake. Many times, these sellers would have been better off continuing with the deal because any new buyer would bring new time and costs to the deal, and they would probably provide a very similar assessment once disclosed with all the information.

On rare occasions, it can be good to pull back. It can provide time for a break, time to fix a diligence or performance issue, and then provide the ability to try to build a new deal. Unfortunately, it is very rare that this is actually the right choice. Normally, what we have seen is that the issues take longer to fix than the seller anticipates, and in that time, they would have been better off having a capital partner that might have been able to help in resolving the issues.

TRAITS OF SUCCESSFUL DEALS

Let's now discuss traits of successful deals. These traits are generally a result of the market allowing the buyer and seller the opportunity to meet.

Attractive growth and ability to scale

Whether simply growing, adding new customers or clients, or looking at an acquisition, if a company has clear and attractive growth, the opportunity will be hard for investors to pass up. Furthermore, when an investor sees a company's ability to further scale, a deal naturally will make even more sense to them.

Mutual expectations

Many successful deals have a combination of momentum and mutual realistic expectations about the future. Those seem to result in a win/win upon an exit. Having a fair deal that both parties are satisfied with allows for a shared excitement and common vision.

Financial

There are also instances where selling is purely a company owner's financial decision relative to their working and personal life. If there is enough money on the table that would equate to 15 or 20 years of work, it becomes a lot more important for a seller to follow through with a sale or a majority deal.

Necessity

Some successful deals occur largely out of necessity. These are usually scenarios where there is a forced transaction either through equity exit timelines, death, divorce, distress, etc.

COMPONENTS OF A PURCHASE AGREEMENT

Let's end this chapter with a quick overview of the typical components of a purchase agreement.

The merger section. Also known as the "Business Combination" section, the merger section describes the basic structure of a transaction and the form of payment to be made.

The letter of transmittal section. This section describes the contents of the letter sent to all of the seller's shareholders explaining the purchase terms and their right to submit their shares for payment, conversion, or to obtain appraisal rights.

The representations and warranties section. This describes a number of conditions to which both buyer and seller parties state they are in compliance. Though it applies to both parties, the real impact is on the seller, who warrants that its actual operations and financial results are as represented to the buyer.

The conduct of business section. This section requires the seller to conduct its business prior to the closing date in the best interests of the buyer.

The additional agreements section. This section includes miscellaneous provisions, such as mutual agreements to news releases and covenants to assist in all steps necessary to complete the transaction.

The closing section. This states the details of when and where the closing will take place.

The termination prior to closing section. This section notes the conditions under which the parties can terminate the transaction prior to closing.

The supporting documents section. This itemizes the documents that each party must receive before the transaction can be completed.

Exhibits and schedules. This section includes a broad array of attachments, such as the seller's articles of incorporation, fixed asset list, shareholder list, and liability and contract itemization.

Chapter 7

AFTER THE CLOSE

One of the biggest mistakes that companies and investors can make is not having an operating plan for what happens after a deal is closed. We typically recommend that a company has a 100-day plan (or a one-year plan) and a three-year plan, and that they have a shared long-term vision for the company. Having those plans in place eases the transition process after the transaction, which is when most of the difficult scenarios occur if expectations are misaligned.

For example, in one company we worked with, the CEO/founder sold a 65 percent stake in his company to an investment group. Part of this stake was for personal liquidity, and the other part was for capital to grow and operate the company. The CEO/founder had expectations that this was a long-term transaction and he would have the ability to run his company for the next three to five years, grow it, and then sell it.

The investor, on the other hand, expected to quickly sell the company to maximize a short-term internal rate of ROI. The latter is what ended up happening, and the investor actually sold the company out from under the CEO. The CEO was quite disappointed because he felt that it was too early to sell the company and that it could have gone through another cycle of growth to reach a much larger purchase price. The investor did not have those same expectations, feelings, and thoughts, hence the earlier-than-expected sale.

In talking with the CEO, we learned that they had never outlined or discussed any 100-day, one-year, or three-year vision for the company.

In another example, we worked with a senior credit facility on a refinance deal. The company was going through a growth phase, unbeknownst to the bank. When we reviewed the financing in place, its line of credit was not scaled or set up to handle the ramp-up time for growth, and neither were the terms and conditions.

Fortunately, this company's growth turned out to be good growth, and the company was able to refinance and increase their line of credit with a new lender, preventing the company from running out of money and allowing it to continue on its growth path. That being said, the line of credit increase was a fairly intense process and one that probably could have been avoided by having a clear 100-day, one-year, or three-year plan in place early on.

Once these plans are in place, the next step is for everyone to simply do their part. If there are agreed-upon plans, it is important that management stick to those plans and deliver results. It is also important that the capital partner respects the results of the management team if they are aligned with the agreed-upon plan. This step can alleviate a lot of pressure and anxiety for all parties and can prevent many company-threatening issues.

HAVE A FINANCIAL PLAN FOR PROCEEDS

In the case of being acquired, it is strongly recommended that sellers have a financial plan in place before closing that outlines what they will do with the money upon closing. I have seen many people go into an exit with a financial plan and be quite pleased with how things worked out. However, there are also examples of those we've seen who received a significant amount of money at close, but had little to no personal financial planning in place. They ended up spending most of the money before they realized that the capital was finite and could have been handled more advantageously.

Here are a couple of good stories along with a tougher story. On the tougher side of things, just before the Great Recession in 2008, a founder I knew well sold his company for north of $20 million. He then invested all the proceeds into a handful of illiquid and varied real estate projects.

When the financial crisis hit, he ended up seeing his 25 years' worth of work become nearly worthless. Situations like this are tough but real. Needless to say, we encourage you to have a diverse financial plan in place regarding how to handle your proceeds from the sale.

On the flip side, there have been many, many clients who got liquidity from their company, had a solid plan for what to do with the funds, and went on to have a fulfilling financial life. One example is a previous client who was part of two successful exits and is now an investor/advisor for lower middle market companies. He keeps a "financial opportunity" door open for himself by investing in interesting and exciting companies, but he also has enough diversification so that if something goes awry, he has other assets that will provide him and his family economic protections.

BE READY FOR CHANGE

The last thing to address post-close is how the company will inevitably be different. Things will never be the same once you bring in an institutional partner. Your company is your life's work, and it can be hard to watch it change, but you need to be prepared that this is inevitable and accept that it is going to change. You should also encourage management to think of ways to handle this change through preparations such as having board meetings prior to the sale, managing the company as if there were a third party watching, getting an audit, and more.

Focus on getting things off to a solid start, even if there are initial frustrations, small issues, or questions. One party may end up faring better or worse than others, and a little bit of laundry might get aired after a deal, but try to keep a level head and stay focused on getting the first 100 days under your belt. This is important for both the investor and capital provider, but it is even more important for the company team, the business, and an owner's emotional health.

CONCLUSION

A fter 24-plus years in the finance business, many of the examples throughout this book are my experiences and lessons that I hope can be beneficial to any company owner, CEO, or leader out there. One of the essential foundations of being human is achieving fulfillment, and the kinds of deals this book details can be some of the most fulfilling events a company can experience.

In many regards, deciding which path to take can also be one of the most important decisions a business leader can make. At some point, every company comes to a fork in the road, where its leader must make one of three choices:

1. Maintain steady, organic internal growth and "keep on keeping on."

2. Look for outside capital for growth or M&A sales.

3. Take on an outside strategic partner for liquidity or an exit.

The horizons are limited only by the creativity of the leader, the management team, the product or service, and the market. As you think about the opportunities your company has today, I encourage you to think outside the box and consider all of the paths we have discussed. Stretch beyond your general strategic plans, look toward new avenues for growth, use new techniques to attract investors in your business, find new strategic partners who can provide liquidity to the company and its shareholders, and ultimately utilize these deals to take your company to the next level to leave a legacy for yourself and your employees, as that truly is "Completing the Deal."

Appendix A

KEY RATIOS AND TERMS

The following are terms used in the book.

Activity—Measure of the firm's efficiency in generating sales with its assets

$$\textbf{Collection Period} = \frac{\text{Accounts Receivable}}{\text{Credit Sales per Day}}$$

$$\textbf{Current Ratio} = \frac{\text{Current Assets}}{\text{Current Liabilities}}$$

$$\textbf{Debt Ratio} = \frac{\text{Total Liabilities}}{\text{Total Assets}}$$

$$\textbf{Debt-to-Equity Ratio} = \frac{\text{Long-Term Debt}}{\text{Shareholders' Equity}}$$

$$\textbf{Equity Multiplier Ratio} = \frac{\text{Long-Term Debt}}{\text{Shareholders' Equity}}$$

$$\text{Fixed Asset Turnover} = \frac{\text{Sales}}{\text{Net Fixed Assets}}$$

$$\text{Gross Profit Margin} = \frac{\text{Gross Profit}}{\text{Sales}}$$

$$\text{Inventory Turnover} = \frac{\text{Cost of Goods Sold}}{\text{Average Inventory}}$$

Leverage—Measure of the firm's degree of indebtedness and its ability to meet long-term obligations

Liquidity—Measure of the firm's ability to meet its short-term obligations

$$\text{Net Profit Margin} = \frac{\text{Net Income}}{\text{Sales}}$$

$$\text{Net Working Capital to Total Assets Ratio} = \frac{\text{Current Assets} - \text{Current Liabilities}}{\text{Total Assets}}$$

$$\text{Operating Leverage} =$$

$$\frac{\text{\# of Units} \cdot (\text{Price per Unit} - \text{Variable Cost per Unit})}{\text{\# of Units} \cdot (\text{Price per Unit} - \text{Variable Cost per Unit}) - \text{Fixed Cost}}$$

$$\text{Price to Earnings Ratio} = \frac{\text{Price per Share of Common Stock}}{\text{Earnings per Share}}$$

Profitability—Measure of the return on assets and equity

$$\text{Return on Assets} = \frac{\text{Net Income}}{\text{Assets}}$$

Appendix A: Key Ratios and Terms

$$\text{Return on Equity} = \frac{\text{Net Income}}{\text{Shareholder Equity}}$$

$$\text{Tangible Book Value} = \text{Total Assets} - \text{Goodwill} - \text{Total Liabilities}$$

$$\text{Times Interest Earned} = \frac{\text{EBIT}}{\text{Interest Cash Coverage Ratio}}$$

$$\text{FCCR (Fixed Charge Coverage Ratio)} = \frac{\text{EBIT} + \text{Lease Payments}}{\text{Interest} + \text{Lease Payments}}$$

$$\text{Total Asset Turnover} = \frac{\text{Sales}}{\text{Total Assets}}$$

$$\text{Units} = \frac{\text{Total Fixed Cost}}{\text{Price per Unit} - \text{Variable Cost per Unit}}$$

$$\text{Quick Ratio} = \frac{\text{Current Assets} - \text{Inventory}}{\text{Current Liabilities}}$$

Appendix B

GROWTH CAPITAL GUIDELINES CHECKLIST

It is important during a capital-raising event to approach the process with an ounce of optimism and a pound of reality. It is more important to build a track record, establish a history of matching words with deeds, and have no surprises. Here is a helpful, quick list for reference:

1. Lay out a strategic growth plan that is well prepared.

2. Establish a capital-raising process that details key aspects to a raise.

3. Pull a solid team together to handle the deal so company management can stay focused on running the business.

4. Prepare prospective investor materials and prepare for meetings. During preparation, it is important to have:

   a. Crisp delivery of your strategy and strategic plan

   b. Detailed knowledge of the market, competitive land-scape, and your company's ability to navigate through the growth

   c. A clear use and timing of deployment of funds

   d. Key relationships, contracts, and levers at the ready to discuss how these items will de-risk the investment

   e. A well-rehearsed management team that is in sync with one another

5. Have a specific capital stack in mind and go to appropriate parties to fill the stack

6. Test the market with early meetings and feedback to make course corrections

7. Approach the process with flexibility to adjustments in valuations, terms, and conditions

8. Plan for two or three alternatives to achieve the desired outcome

Appendix C

DUE DILIGENCE CHECKLIST

Market overview

1. What is the size of the market?

2. How is the market segmented?

3. What is the market's projected growth and profitability?

4. What are the factors affecting growth and profitability?

5. What are the trends in the number of competitors and their size, product innovation, distribution, finances, regulation, and product liability?

Corporate overview

1. When and where was the company founded, and by whom?

2. What is its history of product development?

3. What is the history of the management team?

4. Has the corporate location changed?

5. Have there been ownership changes?

6. Have there been acquisitions or divestitures?

7. What is the company's financial history?

Culture

1. What type of command structure is used? Does it vary by department?

2. Is there a set of standard policies and procedures that govern most processes? How closely do employees adhere to it?

3. What practices does the company use to retain employees?

4. What types of functions do employees engage in as a group, social or otherwise?

5. Does the company generally promote from within or externally?

6. What types of training does the company require of its employees?

7. What types of orientation programs are used for new employees?

8. What types of awards and ceremonies are used to recognize employee achievements?

9. What level of customer service is the company accustomed to providing? Does it support "above and beyond" levels of support and publicize those efforts?

10. What dress code does the company follow? Does this vary by location?

11. What types of feedback mechanisms are used to discuss issues regarding employee performance?

12. How does the company disseminate information to its employees? Is it a formal method, such as a monthly newsletter, or more informal employee meetings?

13. What is the physical environment? Does the company emphasize low costs with cheap furnishings or incentivize performance with more expensive surroundings?

14. Is there a sense of urgency in completing tasks or is the environment more relaxed?

Personnel

1. Obtain a list of all employees, their current compensation, compensation for the prior year, date of hire, date of birth, race, gender, and job titles.

2. Obtain a list of all inactive employees, stating the reason for their inactive status and the prognosis for their return.

3. Obtain copies of the I-9 forms for all active employees.

4. Obtain copies of any employment agreements.

5. Obtain copies of performance evaluation criteria and bonus plans.

6. Obtain copies of any non-compete, intellectual property, and confidentiality agreements. Also obtain copies of non-competes that currently apply to terminated employees.

7. Obtain copies of any salesperson compensation agreements.

8. Obtain copies of any director compensation agreements.

9. Summarize any loan amounts and terms to officers, directors, or employees.

10. Obtain any union labor agreements.

11. Determine the number of states to which payroll taxes must be paid.

12. Obtain a copy of the employee manual.

13. Conduct background checks on principal employees.

14. Summarize the names, ages, titles, education, experience, and professional biographies of the senior management team.

15. Obtain copies of employee résumés.

16. Determine the employee turnover rate for the past two years.

17. Obtain a list of all involuntary terminations within the past year, stating the reason for termination and the age, gender, race, and disability status of each person terminated.

18. Obtain a copy of the organizational chart.

Benefits

1. Review accrued 401(k) benefits. What is the company contribution percentage? What is the level of employee participation?

2. Obtain copies of all pension plan documents, amendments, and letters of determination.

3. Obtain copies of the pension assets, liabilities, expenses, and audits for the past three years.

4. Determine the funding status of the company pension plan and the ten-year projected cash expense associated with it.

5. Itemize all fringe benefits, along with current and projected employee eligibility for participation in each.

6. Obtain a list of all former employees using COBRA coverage and the dates on which their access to COBRA coverage expires.

7. Itemize all executive perquisites above the standard benefits package and the extent of these expenses for the past two years.

Intellectual property

1. Review all current patent, trademark, service mark, trade name, and copyright agreements, and note renewal dates.

2. Obtain an itemization of all pending patent applications.

3. Determine annual patent renewal costs.

4. Determine the current patent-related revenue stream.

5. Document the patent application process. Have any potential patents not been applied for?

6. List all trademark and service mark registrations and pending applications for registration. Verify that all affidavits of use and renewal applications have been filed and prosecution of all pending applications is current.

7. List all unregistered trademarks and service marks used by the organization and dates of any and all registered marks.

8. Collect and catalog copies of all publications and check for unlisted trademarks and service marks and proper notification.

9. List all copyright registrations.

10. List all registered designs.

11. Does the company have any information that provides a competitive advantage? If so, verify that the information is marked as confidential.

12. Have all employees executed invention assignment and confidentiality agreements?

13. Obtain copies of all licenses of intellectual property in which the company is the licensor or the licensee.

14. List all lawsuits pertaining to intellectual property in which the organization is a party.

Brands

1. Review any branding documents. Does the company have a long-term strategic plan for brand support?

2. Review budgeted and actual expenditures for customer support, marketing, and quality assurance related to branding.

3. What types of advertising and promotion are used?

4. Ensure that the company has clear title to any branded names.

5. How well is the brand supported on the company website?

6. Note the amount and trend of any legal fees needed to stop brand encroachment.

Risk management

1. Is there a risk management officer? What is this person's job description?

2. Does the company have an overall risk mitigation plan that it updates regularly?

3. Review all corporate insurance, using a schedule from the company's insurance agency.

4. If there is material pending litigation, determine the extent of the insurance coverage and obtain insurance company confirmation. Note whether insurance terms are for "claims made" or "claims incurred" as well as the amounts of deductibles.

5. Have aggregate insurance amounts been perpetrated, or is there a history of coming close to aggregate totals?

6. Have there been substantial premium adjustments in the past?

7. To what extent does the company self-insure its activities? Are there uninsured risks that the company does not appear to be aware of or is ignoring?

Capacity

1. Determine the facility overhead cost required for minimum, standard, and maximum capacity.

2. Ascertain the amount of capital replacements needed in the near future.

3. Determine the periodic maintenance cost of existing equipment.

4. Determine the maximum sustainable production capacity by production line.

5. Estimate the cost of modifications needed to increase the capacity of each production line or facility.

Assets

1. Verify bank reconciliations for all bank accounts harboring significant cash balances.

2. Obtain current details of accounts receivable.

3. Determine the days of receivables outstanding and the probable amount of bad debt. Review the bad debt reserve calculation.

4. Obtain a list of all accounts and notes receivable from employees.

5. Obtain a list of all inventory items and discuss the obsolescence reserve. Determine the valuation method used.

6. Obtain the current fixed asset listing as well as depreciation calculations. Audit the largest items to verify their existence.

7. Appraise the value of the most expensive fixed assets.

8. Obtain an itemized list of all assets that are not receivables or fixed assets.

9. Ascertain the existence of any liens against company assets.

10. Obtain any maintenance agreements on company equipment.

11. Is there an upcoming need to replace assets?

12. Discuss whether there are any plans to close, relocate, or expand any facilities.

13. Itemize all capitalized research and development or software development expenses.

14. Determine the value of any net operating loss carry-forward assets.

Liabilities

1. Review the current accounts payable listing.

2. Obtain a list of all accounts payable to employees.

3. Review the terms of any lines of credit.

4. Review the amount and terms of any other debt agreements. Review covenants in the debt agreements and determine if the company has breached the covenants in the past or is likely to do so in the near future.

5. Look for unrecorded debt.

6. Verify wage and tax remittances to all government entities and that there are no unpaid amounts.

7. Review the sufficiency of accruals for wages, vacation time, legal expenses, insurance, property taxes, and commissions.

8. Obtain copies of all unexpired purchasing commitments (purchase orders, etc.).

Equity

1. Obtain a shareholder list that notes the number of shares held and any special voting rights.

2. Review all board resolutions authorizing the issuance of stock to ensure that all shares are validly issued.

3. Review all convertible debt agreements to which the company or any subsidiary is a party. Note any restrictions on dividends, incurring extra debt, and issuing additional capital stock. Note any unusual consent or default provisions. Note the conversion trigger points.

4. Review any disclosure documents used in the private placement of securities or loan applications during the preceding five years.

5. Review all documents affecting ownership, voting, or rights to acquire the company's stock for required disclosure and significance to the purchase transactions, such as warrants, options, security holder agreements, registration rights agreements, shareholder rights, or poison pill plans.

Profitability

1. Obtain audited financial statements for the last three years.

2. Obtain monthly financial statements for the current year.

3. Obtain copies of federal tax returns for the last three years.

4. Determine profitability by product, customer, and segment.

5. What are the revenues and profits per employee?

6. What is direct materials expense as a percentage of revenue?

7. How have revenues, costs, and profits been trending for the past three years?

8. How many staff members are directly traceable to the servicing of specific customer accounts?

9. Are there any delayed expenses? Has the customer avoided necessary maintenance expenditures or wage increases in order to boost profitability?

10. Has the company capitalized a disproportionate amount of expenses?

11. Obtain the budgets for the past three years. Does the company routinely achieve its budgets, or does it fall short?

Cash flow

1. Construct a cash forecast for the next six months. Will the company spin off or absorb cash?

2. Review the trend line of work capital for the past year. How is it changing in relation to total sales?

3. Categorize working capital by segment, product line, and customer. What parts of the business are absorbing the most cash?

4. Determine historical and projected capital expenditure requirements. Does the company have enough cash to pay for its capital investment needs?

Customers

1. How concentrated are sales among top customers?

2. What is the distribution of sales among the various products and services?

3. What is the current sales backlog by customer?

4. What is the seasonality of sales? Are sales unusually subject to changes in business cycle?

5. What is the financial condition of key customers? Does it appear that their businesses are sufficiently robust to continue supporting purchases from the company?

6. How long has the company had sales relationships with its key customers?

7. How profitable are each of the key customer accounts? Do any customers require a disproportionate amount of servicing or require special terms and conditions?

8. Itemize any customer contracts that are coming up for renewal and any likely changes to the key terms of those agreements.

9. Is there a history of complaints from any customers? How profitable are the customers who appear to be the most dissatisfied?

10. Obtain a list of all customers who have stopped doing business with the company in the last three years.

Sales activity

1. Determine the amount of ongoing maintenance revenue from standard profiles.

2. Obtain copies of all outstanding proposals, bids, and offers pending award.

3. Obtain copies of all existing contracts for products or services, including warranty and guarantee work.

4. What is the sales strategy (e.g., add customers, increase support, increase penetration into existing customer base, pricing, etc.)?

5. What is the structure of the sales organization? Are there independent sales representatives?

6. Obtain the sales organizational chart.

7. How many sales personnel are in each sales position?

8. What is the sales force's geographic coverage?

9. What is the sales force's compensation, split by base pay and commission?

10. What was the average sales per salesperson for the past year?

11. What was the sales expense per salesperson for the past year?

12. What is the sales projection by product for the next 12 months?

13. In what category or categories do customers fall—end users, retailers, OEMs, wholesalers, or distributors?

14. How many customers are there for each product, industry, and geographic region?

15. What is the average order size?

16. Does the company have an ecommerce presence? If so, do they have a site that accepts online payments and orders? What percentage of total sales comes through this medium?

17. What is the structure of the technical support group? How many people are in it and what is their compensation?

18. Does the company use email for marketing notifications to customers?

19. What are the proportions of sales by distribution channels?

20. To how many customers can the company potentially market its products? What would be the volume by customer?

21. What is the company's market share? What is the trend?

22. Are there new markets in which company products can be sold?

Product development

1. Obtain a list of development projects in the product pipeline. What is the estimated remaining time and expense required to launch each one?

2. What attributes make the company's new products unique?

3. Have any products been in the development pipeline for a long time but have no immediate prospects for product launch?

4. Who are the key development personnel? What is their tenure, experience, technical and educational background?

5. Does the company primarily use incremental product improvements or engage in major new product development projects?

6. How much money is invested annually in development? Is the amount determined based on a proportion of sales? How does this spending compare to that of competitors?

7. Does the company have a history of issuing inadequately engineered products that fail? Is this finding supported by warranty claim records?

8. Is there a product development plan? Does it tend to target low-cost products, ones with special features, or some other strategy? How closely does the development team adhere to it?

9. Does the company use target costing to achieve predetermined profitability targets?

10. Does it design products that avoid constrained resources?

Production process

1. Does the company have a push or pull manufacturing system?

2. Does the company practice constraint management techniques?

3. Does the company use work cells or continuous assembly lines?

4. Is there an adequate industrial engineering staff? Does the company have an ongoing plan for process improvement?

5. What is the production area safety record? What types of problems have caused safety failures in the past?

6. What issues have caused shipping delays in the past?

7. What is the history of product rework, and why have rework problems arisen?

Information technology

1. What systems use third-party software, and which ones use custom-built solutions? Are the third-party systems under maintenance contracts, and are the most recent versions installed?

2. To what degree have third-party systems been modified? Have they been so altered that they can no longer be upgraded?

3. Are users' computers monitored for unauthorized software installations?

4. Are software copies secured and only released with proper authorization?

5. What is the level of difficulty anticipated to integrate the company's database into the buyer's system?

6. Are there adequate backup systems in place with off-site storage, both for the corporate-level databases and for individual computers?

7. What is the level of security required for access to the company's servers?

Internet

1. Does the company use the internet for internal use as an interactive part of operations? What functions are used in this manner?

2. Has the company's firewall ever been penetrated, and how sensitive is the information stored on the company network's publicly available segments?

3. Does the company provide technical support information through its website?

4. Are website usage statistics tracked? If so, how are they used for management decisions?

5. In what way could operational costs decrease if the company's customers interacted with it through the internet?

Legal issues

1. Obtain the articles of incorporation and bylaws. Review the existence of preemptive rights, rights of first refusal, registration rights, or any other rights related to the issuance or registration of securities.

2. Review the bylaws and look for any unusual provisions affecting shareholder rights or restrictions on ownership, transfer, or voting of shares.

3. Obtain certificates of good standing for the company and all significant subsidiaries.

4. Review the articles of incorporation and bylaws of each subsidiary. Determine if there are restrictions on dividends to the company. For each subsidiary, review the minutes of the board of directors for matters requiring disclosure.

5. Obtain a list of all states in which the company is qualified to do business and a list of those states in which it maintains significant operations. Determine if there are any states where the company is not qualified but should be qualified to do business.

6. Obtain the minutes from all shareholder meetings for the past five years. Review for proper notice prior to meetings, the existence of a quorum, and proper voting procedures; verify that stock issuances have been authorized; verify that insider transactions have been approved; verify that officers have been properly elected; verify that shares are properly approved and reserved for stock options and purchase plans.

7. Obtain and review the minutes of the executive committee and audit committee for the past five years, as well as the minutes of any other special board committees. Review all related documents.

8. Review all contracts that are important to operations as well as any contracts with shareholders or officers. In particular, look for the following provisions:

    a. Default or termination provisions

    b. Restrictions on company action

    c. Consent requirements

    d. Termination provisions in employment contracts

    e. Ownership of technology

    f. Cancellation provisions in major supply and customer contracts

    g. Unusual warranties or the absence of protective provisions

9. Obtain copies of all asset leases, and review for term, early payment, and bargain purchase clauses.

10. Obtain copies of all office space lease agreements, and review for term and renewal provisions.

11. Review all related party transactions for the past three years.

12. Review the terms of any outbound or inbound royalty agreement.

13. Was any company software (either used internally or resold) obtained from another company? If so, what are the terms under which the code is licensed? Are there any associated royalty payments?

14. Review all legal invoices for the past two years.

15. Review all pending and threatened legal proceedings to which the company or any of its subsidiaries is a party. Describe principal parties, allegations, and relief sought; this includes any governmental or environmental proceedings. Obtain copies of existing consent decrees and significant settlement agreements relating to the company or its subsidiaries.

16. If the company is publicly held, obtain all periodic filings for the past five years, including the 10-K, 10-Q, 8-K, and schedule 13D.

17. Review all annual and quarterly reports to shareholders.

18. Review the auditor's letter to management concerning internal accounting controls and procedures, as well as any management responses.

19. Review any reports from outside consultants or analysts concerning the company.

20. Read through any press releases or articles about the company within the past year.

21. Review all related party transactions for the past three years.

22. Review the terms of any outbound or inbound royalty agreements.

23. Review title insurance for any significant land parcels owned by the company.

Regulatory compliance

1. Review the company's correspondence with the Securities and Exchange Commission (SEC), any national exchange, or state securities commission, other than routine transmittals, for the past five years. Determine if there are or were any enforcement or disciplinary acquisitions or any ongoing investigations or suggestions of violations by any of these entities.

2. Review any correspondence during the past five years with the EPA, FTC, OSHA, EEOC, or IRS. Determine if there are any ongoing investigations or suggestions of violations by any of these agencies.

3. Review any required regulatory compliance and verify that necessary licenses and permits have been maintained as well as ongoing filings and reports.

4. If there is a general service administration schedule, when does it come up for renewal?

5. Obtain copies of the most recently filed EEO-1 and VETS-100 forms.

6. Obtain copies of affirmative action plans.

7. Obtain copies of any open charges of discrimination, complaints, or related litigation, or any such cases that have been closed within the past five years.

Policies and procedures

1. Obtain the accounting policies and procedures manuals.

2. Review all key accounting policies to ensure that they comply with generally accepted accounting principles.

3. Obtain the standard offer letter format, the standard termination letter format, and the employment application form.

4. Obtain the human resources policies relating to sexual harassment, background investigations, and drug testing.

The purchase transaction

If the transaction involves the issuance of stock, are there sufficient authorized shares for the offering, including any conversion rights taking into account any shares reserved for issuance pursuant to outstanding options, warrants, convertible securities, and employee benefit plans?

Red flag events

1. Has an auditor resigned within the past three years?

2. Is there evidence of continual changes in accounting methods?

3. Are there unusually complex business arrangements that do not appear to have a clear business purpose?

4. Is the company continually exceeding its loan covenant targets by very small amounts?

5. Do any of the principles have criminal records?

6. Has there recently been significant insider stock sales?

7. Is the internal audit team subjected to significant scope restrictions?

8. Is a large proportion of monthly sales completed during the last few days of each month?

9. Has the company tried to sell itself in the past and failed?

10. Has the company received major warnings from regulatory agencies?

11. Does the company appear to manipulate reserve accounts in order to smooth or enhance its reported earnings?

ACKNOWLEDGMENTS

I would like to say thank you to my family, my colleagues, and friends who have helped to make this book a reality, including Jon D'Andrea, Jon Sanfelippo, Liz Schwab, Kevin Brady, Jeremy Mosier, Zach Roschmann, Michael Deschene, and Jordan Markim.

ABOUT THE AUTHOR

Matt Andersen is the CEO of Westlake Securities, an investment bank that is passionate about working with middle market companies to grow their value and create an attractive path to liquidity. He's worked with companies through growth, turnaround, distress, transformational change, and ultimate sale strategies. With over 24 years of experience and over $5 billion in debt, securities, and M&A transactions, he is a noted investment banking industry expert, speaker, and author. As of the writing of this book, he has a board role with five middle market companies whose combined enterprise value is estimated to be in excess of $400 million.

www.ingramcontent.com/pod-product-compliance
Lightning Source LLC
Chambersburg PA
CBHW030512210326
41597CB00013B/885